Ilmar Tammelo

# Modern Logic in the Service of Law

Springer-Verlag
Wien New York

Univ.-Prof. Mag. iur., Dr. iur. Ilmar Tammelo, M. A., LL. M., Institute for Legal Philosophy, Methodology of Legal Sciences, and General Theory of State, University of Salzburg, Austria




Printed in Austria by Ferd. Berger, Horn

Library of Congress Cataloging in Publication Data. Tammelo, Ilmar, 1917 –. Modern logic in the service of law. Bibliography: p. Includes index. 1. Law-Methodology. 2. Law-Philosophy. 3. Logic. I. Title. K213.T345, 340.1, 78–9169

ISBN 3–211–81486–8 Springer-Verlag Wien–New York
ISBN 0–387–81486–8 Springer-Verlag New York–Wien

*To Lyn*

## PREFACE

In face of persistent and notable efforts taking place in many parts of the world today to make modern logic a tool of legal thought, lawyers are inclined to ask: "What is the real significance of modern logic for us?" A summary answer to this question is: "Modern logic provides up-to-date principles and methods for tracing and displaying self-consistent thought, which is indispensable for efficient and proper performance of legal tasks." This answer may not satisfy the questioner's curiosity about modern logic in the service of law. If he wants to know more, he is invited to join in an investigation of the various ways in which modern logic can prove useful in legal thought.

The present book proposes to engage in such an investigation, and in doing so it also endeavors to meet various challenges to legal logic. If the value of this logic is totally denied, a reaction to this denial is to ask what its reasonable alternative could possibly be. So far there appears to be no sensible reply to this question. The merit of many specific criticisms of legal logic is indisputable. Some of them can be adequately met by showing what has been so far achieved and what can still be achieved in the enhancement of the rationality of legal thought by the aid of legal logic. Some criticisms relate to matters which warrant strictures - to defend legal logic does not mean defending everything contained in the works of legal logicians.

Of all the challenges against the contention that modern logic is a valuable tool of legal thought, the following is the most awkward to parry: "Please show me in what particular way modern logic can be useful for lawyers in their actual work!" For meeting this challenge, Ron Klinger, my former associate in Sydney, has suggested the following parable:

> A man who has not been taught otherwise has always walked on all fours. Upon being asked why he does not walk upright, he answers: "I have been walking on all fours for all my life. Why should I change now? I have managed to propel myself quite well in my accustomed way. Please show that walking upright will enable me to do it better. And won't it take a lot of training to walk upright? I do not have time and stamina to start learning this different way of locomotion."

The difference between the lawyer equipped with legal logic and the one not so equipped is as stark as the difference between a man who walks on all fours and a man who walks upright. The arguments adduced by the scoffers of legal logic are basically the arguments of the man on all fours. The above challenge is awkward to parry because the appreciation of the value of modern logic in the service of law necessitates having sufficient training in this logic and acquiring expertise in its application. And this, of course, is the very thing which many lawyers are reluctant or unable to do. So it becomes a virtually impossible task to show the uses and usefulness of modern logic in legal thought to those lawyers who know very little about it and who cannot find time to acquaint themselves with it. Yet, just as the superiority of walking upright is self-evident to those who do so, the superiority of expertise in legal logic is self-evident to those who have it.

The main concern of legal logicians is not with those who shut their minds to and denounce legal logic offhand; their concern is with those who are prepared to be dispassionate and impartial - prepared to give it a fair trial and then to come to a well-founded conclusion. Proceeding from the assumption that modern logic has uses also in lawyers' actual work, this book endeavors to furnish logical treatment of various practical and theoretical legal problems. It tries to show not only that these problems are amenable to such treatment, but also that the search for their rational solution requires it. No doubt, legal reasoning has also a material aspect, in whose treatment the role of logic is subsidiary. However, the total strength of legal reasoning depends on the strength of any of its links, among which the one supplied by legal logic is inseverable and irreplaceable.

This book is not intended to be an introduction to legal logic, as its forerunner *Outlines of Modern Legal Logic* (which I published in 1969) was meant to be. For making full use of it, an acquaintance with *Outlines* or with some recent work on the foundations of general logic is advisable. It does not deal with extensional calculus, nor does it build, like *Outlines*, the foundations of logic on protological calculus. Thus, the number of logical symbols could be reduced and it was possible to concentrate on that part of modern logic which appears to be the most useful for most legal purposes. Accordingly, the theoretical scope of this book is limited to the logic of indicatives. The theoretical foundation of modern logic is constituted here by an axiomatic system. For the purposes of deduction, I have employed mainly the counter-formula method, a novel decision-procedure I developed with Ron Klinger in Sydney and Helmut Schreiner in Salzburg to meet above all the practical needs of legal reasoning. This method has stood the test in research and teaching; a proof of its logical completeness has been provided by Professor Paul Lorenzen of Erlangen. Another novel feature of this book is its logical notation, which is based on the Polish notation, but diverges from it in some respects in order to achieve shorter and better readable formulae.

Legal language, as actually employed in legal instruments and legal arguments, seldom lends itself to logical treatment directly. An essential step for the legal reasoner who applies logic is to convert the given raw material of legal language into the language of logic. This step involves hazards, because distortions of the intended meanings can easily enter into the reformulation. Therefore, this book devotes particular attention to the problem of the relationship between legal language and logical language to pave the way for their mutual rendition. After having thus prepared the ground for the application of modern logic to law and legal reasoning, the book analyses a number of instances of legal thought in the light of this logic. The selection of the legal materials for this purpose has been mainly determined by their amenability to logical treatment without extensive recourse to legal interpretation or construction, whose principles and methods are beyond the scope of this book. The selection has not been determined by legal, political, or ethical importance of materials, but primarily by their illustrative value for logical purposes.

A reader not accustomed to symbolic expressions (which of necessity abound in this book) is likely to experience aversion to them and may even ask whether legal logic *must* be *symbolic* logic. The answer to this question is emphatically affirmative. There can be no efficiently workable logic without an extensive use of symbolic expressions as there can be no efficiently workable mathematics without them. That symbols are employed in logical reasoning does not mean that it is just a variety of mathematical reasoning. Modern logic is more fundamental than mathematics, which is only one of its special applications.

I prepared a preliminary draft for this book in Sydney in 1972 with Ron Klinger as a project sponsored by the Australian Research Grants Committee. The work on Part I of the book was mainly done by me and the work on the first two chapters of Part II was mainly done by him. Because other challenging intellectual tasks called him away and I accepted a call by the University of Salzburg, our common work came to an end. I rewrote the manuscript twice incorporating in it the results of my research in legal logic during the subsequent years. I now assume the sole responsibility for the book and, in agreement with Ron Klinger, it now appears under my name.

Ron Klinger's contributions to this book remain invaluable. In particular I would like to say that it was he who formulated the rules of the counter-formula method in its earliest version and it was he who developed the method of formalization of legal arguments examined here. Further, I have greatly benefited from comments, criticisms, and suggestions by several other lawyers or philosophers, among whom are my wife Lyndall Tammelo, Dr. Georges Kalinowski of Paris, Mr. Fiori Rinaldi of Canberra, Dr. Helmut Schreiner, Professor Ivanhoe Tebaldeschi, Dr. Rudolf Stranzinger, Professor Edgar Morscher of Salzburg, and my American student Robert Taylor. I am particularly indebted to Professor Jean-Louis Gardies of Nantes, who read the prefinal version of the manuscript and who draw my attention to a number of errors and other shortcomings, which had escaped my notice so far. I cannot expect that any of the above named would fully endorse this book; but neither do I myself regard it as consummate. A work of the present kind can be only a step toward the full coverage of its field of inquiry and toward a comprehensive, penetrating and impeccable treatment of all relevant problems.

Salzburg
February, 1978

Ilmar Tammelo

## Table of Contents

## LIST OF ABBREVIATIONS

| | |
|---|---|
| A.A.C. | Autological Adjunction Contraction (or Autological A-Junction Contraction) |
| A.C. | Adjunction Contraction (or A-Junction Contraction) |
| Add. | Addition |
| A.E. | Adjunction Elimination (or A-Junction Elimination) |
| Ass. | Association |
| Asym. | Asymmetry |
| Aut. | Autology |
| Barb. | *Modus Barbara* |
| Baro. | *Modus Baroco* |
| B.Diss. | Bijunction Dissection |
| Boc. | *Modus Bocardo* |
| Bram. | *Modus Bramantip* |
| CA.Dual. | Contraadjunction Duality (or Contra-A-Junction Duality) |
| C.A.E. | Conjunctive Adjunction Elimination |
| Camen. | *Modus Camenes* |
| Cames. | *Modus Camestres* |
| CB.Diss. | Contrabijunction Dissection |
| C.C. | Conjunction Contraction |
| C.C.D. | Complex Constructive Dilemma |
| CC.Dual. | Contraconjunction Duality |
| C.D.D. | Complex Destructive Dilemma |
| C.D.Dual. | Contradejunction Duality |
| C.E. | Conjunction Elimination |
| CE.Diss. | Contra-E-Junction Dissection |
| CI.Dual. | Contra-I-Junction Duality |
| Cel. | *Modus Celarent* |
| Ces. | *Modus Cesare* |
| CF | Counter-formula |
| CFC | Counter-formula of the Conclusion |

| | |
|---|---|
| CFM | Counter-formula Method |
| C.M. | *Consequentia Mirabilis* |
| CO.Dual. | Contra-O-Junction Duality |
| Comm. | Commutation |
| Conv. | Conversity |
| CS.Dual. | Contrasubjunction Duality |
| CU.Dual. | Contra-U-Junction Duality |
| Dara. | *Modus Darapti* |
| Darii | *Modus Darii* |
| Dat. | *Modus Datisi* |
| D.Dual. | Dejunction Duality |
| D.E. | Dyslogy Elimination |
| Dim. | *Modus Dimaris* |
| Dis. | *Modus Disamis* |
| Diss. | Dissection |
| Distr. | Distribution |
| D.N. | Double Negation |
| D.T.P. | Dyslogy Test Proviso |
| Dual. | Duality |
| ECF | Extended Counter-formula |
| E.Diss. | E-Junction Dissection |
| E.R. | Elimination Rule |
| Exp. | Exportation |
| F-CF | Formula Counter-formula |
| Fel. | *Modus Felapton* |
| Ferio. | *Modus Ferio* |
| Feris. | *Modus Ferison* |
| Fesa. | *Modus Fesapo* |
| Fest. | *Modus Festino* |
| F.Q. | *Ex Falso Quodlibet* |
| Fre. | *Modus Fresison* |
| H.S. | Hypothetic Syllogism |
| I.A.C. | Insertion of the Antecedent of Conclusion |
| I.C. | Inserted Conclusion |
| Id. | Identity |
| I.Dual. | I-Junction Duality |
| Inconv. | Inconversity |
| Intrans. | Intransitivity |

| | |
|---|---|
| I.P. | Indirect Proof |
| I.R. | Identity Relationship |
| Irrefl. | Irreflexivity |
| M.P. | *Modus Ponens* |
| M.P.P. | *Modus Ponendo Ponens* |
| M.P.T. | *Modus Ponendo Tollens* |
| M.T. | *Modus Tollens* |
| M.T.P. | *Modus Tollendo Ponens* |
| M.T.T. | *Modus Tollendo Tollens* |
| N.-asym. | Non-asymmetry |
| N.C. | Negation of Conclusion |
| N.Ct. | Non-contradiction |
| N.-p.sym. | Non-parasymmetry |
| N.-sym. | Non-symmetry |
| O.A.C. | O-Junctive Adjunction Contraction |
| O.E. | O-Junction Elimination |
| P.conv. | Paraconversity |
| P.D.F. | Principle of Derivation Form |
| Perm. | Permutation |
| P.N. | Particulizer Negation |
| P.refl. | Parareflexivity |
| P.sym. | Parasymmetry |
| P.T. | Particular Stigmication |
| P.trans. | Paratransitivity |
| P.Y. | Particular Synopication |
| Q.L. | Quantor Location |
| Q.S. | Quantor Subordination |
| Q.V. | *Ex Quolibet Verum* |
| R.C. | Rule of Conjunction |
| R.D. | Rule of Detachment |
| Refl. | Reflexivity |
| R.P.R. | Rule of Position Rearrangement |
| R.R. | Rule of Replacement |
| R.S. | Rule of Substitution |
| S.C.D. | Simple Constructive Dilemma |
| S.D.D. | Simple Destructive Dilemma |
| S.Dual. | Subjunction Duality |
| SQS | Semantic Quality Sign('s) |

| | |
|---|---|
| S.R. | Sparing Rule |
| STM | Short-cut Tabular Method |
| Sub. | Subordination |
| Sym. | Symmetry |
| T.C. | Transformed Conclusion |
| T.I. | Tautology Insertion |
| T.n.D. | *Tertium non Datur* |
| T.R. | Transcription Rule |
| Trans. | Transitivity |
| Transp. | Transposition |
| U.Dual. | U-Junction Duality |
| U.N. | Universalizer Negation |
| WFEF | Well-formed Predicational Formula |
| WFOF | Well-formed Propositional Formula |

INTRODUCTION

A book whose title is *Modern Logic in the Service of Law* is expected to deal with *some* techniques of legal reasoning. Could it deal with *all* techniques of it? Legal reasoning certainly purports to be a rational enterprise; however, it definitely is not wholly and solely logical reasoning if logic is conceived as a discipline of thought concerned only with the formal aspect of reasoning. Uses of the word "logic" which embrace principles and methods of all sorts of rational procedures occur mainly among those who are not experts in logic. These uses abound also in legal literature. It is not advisable to follow this historically and etymologically founded but none the less doubtful practice. To achieve a proper demarcation of various disciplines of thought from which lawyers may find the intellectual tools they need in their work, various modes of legal reasoning are to be distinguished. In line with a vast majority of contemporary logicians, the word "logic" is employed in the present book to signify that discipline which examines and provides those principles and methods by means of which formally sound reasoning can be established and secured.

It may be asked whether legal logic constitutes a special logic, and if so, then in what sense. The adjective "legal" suggests that this logic is, indeed, a special kind of logic; but the phrase "special logic" itself alludes that it cannot be a logic in conflict with general logic; for the special is but an instance of the general. Therefore, what is sometimes called "a special logic of common law" can mean - if the word "logic" is to retain an acceptable sense in this phrase - only general logic applied in the field of common law. Those who employ this phrase appear to have in mind not logic properly so called. They refer perhaps to modes of reasoning peculiar to common-law learning, that is, to certain informal rational procedures which fall beyond the scope of logic in the logicians' sense and which, if sound, in no way conflict with principles and methods of general logic. It is to be emphasized that modern legal logic can have no substitute in a non-logic. This is not to deny that there are good habits or patterns of lawyers' reasonings whose logical structure is not obvious, but which nevertheless conform to logically sound reasoning. This implicit, "common-sense" logic may be sufficient for most practical purposes. However, when there is any doubt as to the formal validity or solidity of instances of legal reasoning, there is no escape from recourse to appropriate methods of modern logic in order to attain a certainty about this validity or solidity.

Formal validity means that an argument holds independently of any particular content of thought in its premiss or premisses or in its conclusion. Logic, whose procedures take their course in the abstraction of the material aspect of thought, can therefore be called "formal logic" to emphasize a characteristic feature of logical reasoning, bearing in mind that "formal" is a gratuitous addition when "logic" is used in the technical sense of the word. Formal impeccability is a precondition of self-consistent reasoning. It is indisputable that in the field of law, as elsewhere, self-consistency is a most important aim - a standard for all aspects of lawyers' work performed in the spirit of their professional ethics. Legal reasoning as a rational enterprise is not limited to formal aspects of legal thought. Another essential task of it is the discovery and substantiation of materially sound legal thought-formations. The totality of this latter kind of reasoning can be called "zetetic", to introduce for a useful function a rarely used word of Greek origin. Hence, legal reasoning can be divided into logical reasoning and zetetic reasoning.

Logical reasoning is deductive in the sense that the application of appropriate principles of inference leads to conclusions that necessarily follow from the given premisses. This reasoning does not itself guarantee the material soundness of the claimed conclusions, but it contributes to the achievement of it. In a logically valid inference, the conclusion must be also materially sound if its premisses are free from contradictions and materially sound. From the formal point of view, which is relevant to logic, the results of logical reasoning can be regarded as completely certain. This means that the principles and methods of logic applied in formal reasoning are "fixed" for the purposes of this reasoning and can therefore be resorted to without questioning in the course of execution of logical procedures. Nevertheless, on the level of the foundations of logic some of its ideas may be called in question. Challenges to the existing systems of logic are not excluded and may be successful, which may lead to improvements or refinements of ideas or techniques of logic. Where in the course of application of logic results are obtained which appear unsound, the source of unsoundness can lie in a faulty application of the formal instruments employed, or in an improper choice of the premisses used, or in defects in the material on which this reasoning operates in the given instances. Only the first source is a direct concern of logicians.

In contrast to logical reasoning, zetetic reasoning is non-deductive. It never leads to formally necessary conclusions. Formally, the conclusions here are only possible, that is, without following from their premisses, they do not contradict them. Thus, for the generalizations achieved by inductive methods only a degree of probability can be claimed. In reasoning by analogy, in which conclusions drawn are based on the similarity of relevant factors, only verisimilitude can be claimed for the conclusions. For the conclusions that are reached by those methods by which value judgments are justified, merely plausibility can be claimed. From the formal point of view, the conclusions reached by zetetic reasoning are not cogent, unless a general principle is superadded to instances of such reasoning - one capable of converting them into instances of deductive reasoning.

To equip the lawyer with adequate knowledge of all he requires for the multiple functions of his reasoning, a full exposition of the principles and method of logical as well as zetetic reasoning is required. The present book does not propose to enter into all kinds or aspects of legal reasoning. It concentrates only on problems of *logic* confronting this reasoning.

The system of logic on which applications of logic to legal problems is based in this book is a system of two-valued logic operating with the concepts "true" and "false". These values, conceived as "formally true" and "formally false" or as "*ex hypothesi* true" and "*ex hypothesi* false", are ascribed to indicative thought-formations, viz. to propositions or to predications. There are notable attempts to apply systems of multi-valued logic, especially those of three-valued logic, to the treatment of legal problems and attempts to analyze law itself by systems of non-indicative thought-formations. Both attempts are interesting and potentially significant; however, (with a few exceptions) their practical usefulness is not yet established. They are still under scrutiny; contingencies and difficulties in their application are not yet sufficiently canvassed.

The present book keeps as close as possible to what is well settled in the theory of logic and has withstood tests in practice. By means of the tools of thought which the established theory of indicative logic sets at lawyers' disposal, most problems of self-consistency in legal reasoning can be solved. The logic of classes, which has an important application in the field of law (and which was sketched in my *Outlines of Modern Legal Logic* in the framework of extensional calculus) is not included here. Thoughts framed as class concepts can be handled by instruments of predicational calculus, since it is possible to give them an intensional interpretation.

Since the thought-formations subjected to logical treatment in this book are indicative, the question arises as to how the logical equipment here to be supplied can be applied to thought *within* law itself as distinguished from thought *about* law. The legal norms appear not to assert something; they rather call for something. They are directives rather than indicatives. Whatever the names of the logical values appropriate to them may be, these surely cannot be "true" and "false" in the ordinary sense. Ascription of logical values other than those peculiar to indicatives seems to be required when law is viewed from within a given legal system. When law is viewed from outside a given legal system, it is possible to make assertions about legal norms, and these assertions can be regarded as either true or false; for law is a kind of reality and it is always possible to make true or false statements about an instance of reality.

Any true statement about the existence of a legal norm imports that there is a legal norm having the contents signified by the corresponding assertion. Given a legal norm, it is to be assumed that there is also a directive to its addressee or addressees, a call to behave in the manner specified in the legal norm. Any false statement about the existence of a legal norm imports that there is no legal norm having the contents indicated by the corresponding assertion; accordingly, it cannot be assumed in this case that there is a legal directive calling upon its addressee or addressees to behave in the manner specified in the legal norm.

For the purposes of logical treatment of law, any legal norm can be captured by an ought-, may-, or can-assertion whose indicative *form* is meant to carry a directive *force* (expressible by the imperative sentence "Act accordingly!" referring to the relevant indicative sentence). What the logical values appropriately to be ascribed to thought-formations employed in formal reasoning are is a question, often vexing, which can be side-stepped by resorting to the axiomatic method in the construction of logic. The observance logical theses established in this way assures formal validity of all stringent arguments and there is no need for ascribing any particular logical value to the thought-formations as a precondition of their logical treatment. This consideration has been one that has led to the construction of the system of logic underlying the subsequent expositions as an axiomatic system. The logical formulae which occur in this book are capable of being interpreted also as representing non-indicative thought-formations; their expressions should be furnished by appropriate key-signs, for example, "!" for imperatives and "?" for interrogatives.

There is a widespread and obdurate opinion among lawyers that logic understood as a formal discipline fetters them in their efforts to achieve desirable legal results - not only to achieve professional success, but also to attain justice and common good through law. This book will try to dispel this impression by showing that, contrary to popular suspicions, modern logic in the service of law has a liberating effect on the legal mind. Logical treatment of legal problems will help to determine the areas of choices available for the legal decision-maker and show that these are often less limited than is ordinarily assumed. It will properly open up the areas in which zetetic reasoning has a legitimate scope and will thus make the legal reasoner free from prejudices engendered by the spurious authority of pseudo-logical habits obfuscating vision of values and interfering with his passing apposite value judgments.

# Part I

# Theoretical Foundations of Legal Logic

# I. A System of Propositional Calculus

## 1. *Preliminary Considerations about Propositional Calculus*

The theoretical foundation of the legal logic developed and applied in the present book lies in the system of propositional calculus here to be constructed. This calculus is expressed in a formalized language of symbols to be introduced and explained. It provides for devices by means of which logical aspects of legal thought can be expressed as formulae; it also provides for the derivation schemata by the aid of which logically sound legal inferences can be made and formal qualities of legal arguments can be ascertained. The system of the calculus will be constructed as an axiomatic system.

The formalization and axiomatization to be effected here relate only to the instruments of thought designed for the treatment of the formal aspect of legal thought. The effort to assure the rigour of the enterprise of producing these instruments leaves the substance of legal thought itself intact. In no way does it impose a rigidity or formalism on law or its administration. It is nothing else but a resolute attempt to gain an impeccable basis for shaping, handling, and judging instances of legal thought from the formal point of view and by means of logical methods.

The discipline of thought concerned with formalized languages of signs such as logical calculi is called "semiotics". The totality of the instructions for constructing a calculus is a logical syntax. It is examined by a branch of semiotics called "syntactics". Another branch concerned with the interpretation of the signs and formulae in a calculus is called "semantics". A further branch concerned with the relation of the signs and formulae in a calculus, to their users, is called "pragmatics". The first part of this book deals mainly with syntactic problems; semantic and pragmatic problems will be discussed mainly in its second part.

The calculus itself represents the "object-language" of logic. In order to construct and operate a calculus, various statements relating to its contents have to be made. These statements are expressed in the "meta-language" of logic. This language is not wholly formalized here, but appears as ordinary English with the addition of some symbols when required.

The propositional calculus here to be constructed is based on established logical theory. No special attempt will be made in the course of its exposition to justify its pertinence or usefulness for self-consistent reasoning. That it is reliable for the given purposes has been shown by the vast experience gained in its application in various areas of rational endeavor. However, in order to promote the understanding of its principles and methods and their intelligent application, various problems of the treatment of the calculus will be discussed in the second part of the book.

The present system of propositional calculus consists of the following: (1) *primitives*, which are the smallest units of the system subjected to logical treatment; (2) *operators*, which are the means for the creation of further units of the system; (3) *rules of formation*, which lay down the conditions under which units are admitted in the system; (4) *definitions*, which express certain units in terms of other units; (5) *axioms*, which constitute those basic units of the system from which its other units can be derived; (6) *rules of transformation*, which lay down the modes of derivation in the system. The units derived within the system constitute its *theorems*. A unit which is either an axiom or a theorem of the system is its *thesis*.

What is a definition, an axiom, a rule of transformation, or a theorem in a system of propositional calculus is to some extent optional. Thus various systems of this calculus have been provided, each of which satisfy the basic requirements of axiomatization and produce the same logical results. A guiding idea in constructing axiomatic systems is that of frugality of thought and expression. An axiomatic system is expected to have the following basic features:

(1) The system must be self-consistent, that is, it must not admit a unit and the negation of that unit in it.

(2) The system should be complete, that is, it should be such that any unit admitted in it can be derived in it.

(3) The system should have independent axioms, that is, it should be such that no axiom of it can be derived from any other axiom or axioms of it.

Requirement (1) is peremptory. A system which does not comply with it would admit derivation of any unit and its negation and would thus promote chaos rather than order in reasoning. Requirements (2) and (3) are mandatory. A system which does not comply with them would still be useful as a basic framework for formal reasoning, but would not be an ideal system: a system with incomplete axioms would be of limited application and a system with non-independent axioms would lack elegance. However, a system which contains a redundant axiom may be more convenient for deriving theorems than a system which has independent axioms and thus it may be better suited for practical purposes.

The present system employs the following signs:

(1) Small romans of ordinary size (e.g. p, q, r), which stand for propositional variables; they symbolize any proposition whatsoever that is not formed by a propositional operation.

(2) Small romans of reduced size, (e.g. a, c, m), which stand for propositional instances; they symbolize determinate propositions that are not formed by a propositional operation.

(3) Capital romans of large size (e.g. A, K, E), which stand for junctors (i.e. dyadic propositional operators); they symbolize factors which link propositions into propositional compounds.

(4) A bar on top of any of the above letters (e.g. $\bar{p}$, $\bar{E}$), which stands for the only monadic operator employed in

the present system; it symbolizes a factor negating propositions.

The propositional operators belong to the category of logical *functors*, whereas the propositional variables and the propositional instances belong to the category of logical *fungenda*. "Fungendum" is a neologism introduced here in order to provide a technical term for what is governed by a logical functor. The combinations of the propositional functors (viz. operators) and propositional fungenda (viz. operanda) which satisfy the rules of formation of propositional calculus belong to the category of logical *functions*.

## 2. *The Rules of Formation of Propositional Calculus*

The rules of formation of propositional calculus serve for determining whether a sign or a combination of signs constitutes an admissible unit of the system of this calculus. A sign or a combination of signs which satisfies the conditions laid down in these rules is called a "well-formed propositional formula", here abbreviated as "WFOF". The rules of formation of the present system are:

An expression is a WFOF if it is exactly either

(1) a small roman with or without a subscript attached to it; or

(2) any such expression with any number of bars on its top; or

(3) any expression so formed that one of the following capital romans: C, A, K, E, D, immediately precedes any two WFOFs; or

(4) any expression so formed that one of these capital romans with any number of bars on its top immediately precedes two WFOFs.

For the construction of the present axiomatic system, only small romans of ordinary size are employed. Minuscle arabic numbers are employed as subscripts.

The word "literal" is used here for any letter sign, with or without a subscript or with or without a bar or bars. Accordingly, there are small literals and capital literals. Subscripts used in propositional calculus serve to increase the number of letters which the alphabet can supply. They are required only in the application of logic to propositional instances. It is customary to employ the letters p , q , and those immediately following them in the alphabet for the construction of propositional calculus. It is better to avoid the use of letters such as h , l , and t , for they do not blend well with letters such as p , q , and r when bars are required.

Examples of WFOFs:

Under Rule (1): p , q , r

Under Rule (2): $\overline{p}$ , $\overline{\overline{q}}$ , $\overline{\overline{\overline{r}}}$

Under Rule (3): $C p q$ , $K p E \overline{q} r$ , $A D \overline{p} q K \overline{\overline{r}} C s \overline{\overline{\overline{\overline{v}}}}$

Under Rule (4): $\overline{\overline{E}} p q$ , $\overline{\overline{\overline{A}}} p \overline{K} q \overline{r}$   $\overline{C} C E \overline{p} \overline{\overline{q}} \overline{\overline{\overline{K}}} A r \overline{s} \overline{\overline{E}} s \overline{\overline{\overline{\overline{v}}}} q$

Any WFOF consisting of one small literal constitutes an *elementary propositional formula*. Any such formula having only one bar on top, likewise any two such formulae preceded by one capital roman constitutes a *simple compound propositional formula*. All other WFOFs constitute *complex compound propositional formulae*. Accordingly, as propositional formulae, p is elementary, $\overline{p}$ and $C p q$ are simple compound, and $C p \overline{\overline{q}}$ and $C p \overline{K} \overline{q} r$ are complex compound.

An elementary formula is always a WFOF. In all other cases, the following rule furnishes a convenient test for ascertaining whether or not a formula is a WFOF:

> If the total number of small literals in a formula minus the total number of capital literals equals one then the formula is a WFOF, provided that the formula starts with a capital literal and that the number of small literals to the right of capital literals exceeds the number of such capital literals at any point in the formula.

The simplest way of applying this test is to count up the small literals and then to subtract the number of capital literals. If the answer is not one, it is already proved that the formula is not a WFOF. If the answer is one, it is necessary to check, commencing from the right hand side, that the number of small literals to the right of any capital literal exceeds the number of capital literals at all times.

Apart from the capital literals employed in the present system, WFOFs can be linked here for a special purpose also with the sign " $\leftrightarrow$ " . This sign belongs to logical metalanguage. Its meaning will be explained in the subsequent section, in which it will be employed in the definitions of an axiomatic system.

The special meanings which the propositional operators have are the following: " $\bar{}$ " signifies the operator of negation; it may be called "negator". " C " signifies the operator of subjunction (this is often called "material implication", "extensive implication", or simply "implication"); it may be called "subjunctor". " A " signifies the operator of adjunction (this is often called "inclusive disjunction", "alternation", or simply "disjunction"); it may be called "adjunctor". " K " signifies the operator of conjunction; it may be called "conjunctor". " E " signifies the operator of bijunction (this is often called "equivalence", "coimplication", or "biconditional"); it may be called "bijunctor". " D " signifies the operator of dejunction (this is often called "intensive implication" or "replication"); it may be called "dejunctor".

Special names can also be assigned for the operators with a bar on top. Thus $\bar{C}$ may be called "contrasubjunctor", $\bar{A}$ "contraadjunctor", " $\bar{K}$ " "contraconjunctor", " $\bar{E}$ " "contrabijunctor", and " D " "contraadjunctor". Accordingly, the names of the corresponding functions are "contrasubjunction", "contraadjunction", etc.

With alternatives and caveats to be discussed in Part II, the meanings of the above operators can be rendered as follows:

$\bar{}$ : "it is not that ..."
C : "if ... then ..."
A : "... or ..."
K : "... and ..."
E : "exactly if ... then ..."
D : "only if ... then ..."
$\bar{C}$ : "... without ..."
$\bar{A}$ : "neither ... nor ..."
$\bar{K}$ : "... not with ..."

$\bar{E}$ : "either ... or ..."

$\bar{D}$ : "not ... but ..."

### 3. An Axiomatic System of Propositional Calculus

The axiomatic system of propositional calculus employs only formulae admitted in it as well-formed. The interrelationships of its simple compound formulae are determined by definitions. It is based on postulates called "axioms", from which derivations are made according to rules of transformation. The system here to be constructed contains four axioms, four definitions, and four rules of transformation. It is possible to construct an axiomatic system of propositional calculus with a more reduced number of all these, even with a single axiom and a single rule of transformation. The reduction of the basic instrumentarium may not lead, however, to economy of thought and expression. Thus a system which employs only one operator and thus does not require definitions of simple compound formulae, proves to be extremely cumbersome. The basic instrumentarium of the present system was selected in order to have a system which is relatively easy to grasp and to handle, albeit the axioms chosen are not independent. It is possible to derive Axiom 3 as a theorem, but the derivation of this theorem is very laborious and not warranted in a book which is to serve practical purposes.

*Axioms:*

Ax.1: $C A p p p$

Ax.2: $C p A p q$

Ax.3: $C A p q A q p$

Ax.4: $C C p q C A r p A r q$

In the definitions below, the meta-logical sign "$\leftrightarrow$" is employed. It indicates that the formulae connected with it are interchangeable.

*Definitions:*

Df.1: $C p q \leftrightarrow A \bar{p} q$

Df.2: $D p q \leftrightarrow A p \bar{q}$

Df.3: $K p q \leftrightarrow \bar{A} \bar{p} \bar{q}$

Df.4: $E p q \leftrightarrow \bar{A} \bar{A} \bar{p} q \bar{A} p \bar{q}$

*Rules of Transformation:*

| | |
|---|---|
| Rule of Substitution (R.S.): | In any definition, axiom, or theorem, any WFOF can be uniformly substituted for any variable there occurring. |
| Rule of Replacement (R.R.): | In any WFOF, a component of a definition or a component of a bijunction can be replaced with the other component. |
| Rule of Detachment (R.D.): | If a subjunction and its antecedent are posited then the consequent of this subjunction can be posited. |
| Rule of Conjunction (R.C.): | If two WFOFs are posited then their conjunction can be posited. |

In the above rules, "a component of a definition" means "a WFOF occurring on either side of $\leftrightarrow$ ", "a component of a bijunction" means "a WFOF governed by a bijunctor", "antecedent" means "the first WFOF of a subjunction", and "consequent" means "the second WFOF of a subjunction".

Besides the above instrumentarium, the operation of the present axiomatic system requires the following:

Principle of Derivation Form (P.D.F.):

In every derivation, the derivation base and any formula derived can be integrated into a subjunction whose antecedent is the derivation base and whose consequent is the derived formula.

If a derivation proceeds from a single formula, this formula alone constitutes the derivation base; if it proceeds from several formulae, the conjunction of these formulae constitutes the derivation base.

In the following, samples of theorem derivations are provided for propositional calculus. These derivations appear in the form of derivation schemata. The derivation bases represent the antecedents of subjunctions; the derivates represent consequents of these subjunctions. The ultimate derivates represent the theorems to be proved.

A derivation schema is set out as follows: Where the derivation base consists only of an axiom or axioms, it is not stated. If it contains a formula other than an axiom, this formula is stated; should there be more than one such premiss, they are written on separate lines. The entries in the left hand column of the schema, be they premisses or derivates, are numbered consecutively. The theorem to be derived is written on the top of the right hand column. It is underlined and preceded by the sign " /- ", which belongs to logical meta-language and can be read as "yields". The entries under the line provide the reason for each step of derivation in an abbreviated form. The abbreviations employed are those of axioms, definitions, rules of transformation, theorems derived prior to the instant derivation, or the principle of derivation form. In front of the abbreviation that indicates the reason for a step of derivation, there may occur a number or numbers indicating the entry or entries in the left hand column on which the step rests. The last entry in this column represents the theorem derived; it must therefore be identical with the formula placed on the top of the right hand column.

The following are samples of deduction for deriving theorems in the present axiomatic system:

Th.1: /- $\underline{CCqrCCpqCpr}$

1. $CCqrCA\bar{p}qA\bar{p}r$ — Ax.4, R.S.
2. $CCqrCCpqCpr$ — 1, Df.1, R.R.

In the above derivation, the reason for Step 1 is Axiom 4 (viz. $CCpqCArpArq$) and the Rule of Substitution (under which $q$ is substituted for $p$, $r$ for $q$, and $\bar{p}$ for $r$, wherever the latter occur). Step 2 rests on Step 1, to wit by virtue of the definition $Cpq \leftrightarrow Apq$; the formulae $A\bar{p}q$ and $A\bar{p}r$ are replaced with the formulae $Cpq$ and $Cpr$ respectively.

Th.2:

1. $Cpq$
2. $Cqr$ /- $\underline{CKCpqCqrCpr}$
3. $CCqrCCpqCpr$ — Th.1
4. $CCpqCpr$ — 3,2, R.D.

5. C p r — 4,1, R.D.

6. K C p q C q r — 1,2, R.C.

7. C K C p q C q r C p r — 6,5, P.D.F.

In this derivation, Step 5 produces the consequent of a subjunction whose antecedent, produced by Step 6, represents the derivation base. Accordingly, the reason for Step 7 is the principle of derivation form.

Th.3: /- C p p

1. C p A p p — Ax.2, R.S.
2. K C p A p p C A p p p — 1, Ax.1, R.C.
3. C K C p A p p C A p p p C p p — Th.2, R.S.
4. C p p — 3,2, R.D.

Th.4: /- $A p \bar{p}$

1. C p p — Th.3.
2. $A \bar{p} p$ — 1, Df.1
3. $C A \bar{p} p A p \bar{p}$ — Ax.3, R.S.
4. $A p \bar{p}$ — 3,2, R.D.

Th.5: /- $C p \bar{\bar{p}}$

1. $A p \bar{\bar{\bar{p}}}$ — Th.4, R.S.
2. $C p \bar{\bar{p}}$ — 1, Df.1, R.R.

Th.6: /- $C C p q C \bar{q} \bar{p}$

1. C p q
2. $C q \bar{\bar{q}}$ — Th.5, R.S.
3. $K C p q C q \bar{\bar{q}}$ — 1,2, R.C.
4. $C K C p q C q \bar{\bar{q}} C p \bar{\bar{q}}$ — Th.2, R.S.
5. $C p \bar{\bar{q}}$ — 4,3, R.D.
6. $A p \bar{\bar{\bar{q}}}$ — 5, Df.1, R.R.

7. $C A \bar{p} \bar{\bar{q}} A \bar{\bar{q}} \bar{p}$ — Ax.3, R.S.

8. $A \bar{\bar{q}} \bar{p}$ — 7,6, R.D.

9. $C \bar{q} \bar{p}$ — 8, Df.1, R.R.

10. $C C p q C \bar{q} \bar{p}$ — 1,9, P.D.F.

## 4. *A Catalog of Theses of Propositional Calculus*

Some theses of propositional calculus prove to be particularly useful in deductive inferences. In this section a list of those theses is provided which serve the purposes of legal reasoning. Additional theses will be supplied later where required.

Each selected thesis or group of them carries a name with a corresponding abbreviation. The abbreviations are convenient especially for stating the reasons for the steps of deductive inferences. There is no uniformity in the nomenclature of the theses supplied. The names and abbreviations that will be employed here are mainly those which are most frequently found in the literature of logic. However, some of the listed theses carry the names, with the corresponding abbreviations, which have proved to be suitable for the counter-formula decision-procedure - a main feature of the present book. Thus "Simplification" will be called here "Conjunction Elimination". The list below contains theses that appear in the basic instrumentarium of the above axiomatic system as well as theses that can be derived as theorems.

| | *Name* | *Abbreviation* | *Formula* |
|---|---|---|---|
| 1. | Non-contradiction | N.Ct. | $\bar{K} p \bar{p}$ |
| 2. | *Tertium non Datur* | T.n.D. | $\bar{E} p \bar{p}$ |
| 3. | Identity | Id. | $E p p$ |
| 4. | Double Negation | D.N. | $E p \bar{\bar{p}}$ |
| 5. | Autology | Aut. | $E A p p p$ |
| 6. | Addition | Add. | $C p A p q$ |

| | | | |
|---|---|---|---|
| 7. | Commutation | Comm. | $EApqAqp$ |
| | | | $EKpqKqp$ |
| | | | $EEpqEqp$ |
| 8. | Transposition | Transp. | $ECpqC\bar{q}\bar{p}$ |
| 9. | Duality | Dual. | $ECpqA\bar{p}q$ |
| | | | $EDpqAp\bar{q}$ |
| | | | $EApq\bar{K}\bar{p}\bar{q}$ |
| | | | $EKpq\bar{A}\bar{p}\bar{q}$ |
| 10. | Association | Ass. | $EApAqrAApqr$ |
| | | | $EKpKqrKKpqr$ |
| 11. | Distribution | Distr. | $EKpAqrAKpqKpr$ |
| | | | $EApKqrKApqApr$ |
| 12. | Permutation | Perm. | $ECpCqrCqCpr$ |
| 13. | Exportation | Exp. | $ECKpqrCpCqr$ |
| 14. | Dissection | Diss. | $EEpqKCpqCqp$ |
| | | | $E\bar{E}pqKC\bar{p}qCp\bar{q}$ |
| 15. | Conjunction Elimination | C.E. | $CKpqp$ |
| | | | $CKpqq$ |
| 16. | Subordination | Sub. | $CKpqCpq$ |
| | | | $CKpqApq$ |
| | | | $CKpqEpq$ |
| | | | $CEpqCpq$ |
| 17. | *Modus Ponens* | M.P. | $CKCpqpq$ |
| 18. | *Modus Tollens* | M.T. | $CKCpq\bar{q}\bar{p}$ |
| 19. | Adjunction Elimination | A.E. | $CKApq\bar{p}q$ |
| | | | $CKApq\bar{q}p$ |
| 20. | Hypothetic Syllogism | H.S. | $CKCpqCqrCpr$ |

The list of theses for the use of deductive inferences can be much shorter than the above list, but it can also be longer. A smaller number of theses would entail a more laborious deduction, because some requisite steps would then be possible only through further derivations in the course of actual inferences. A larger number of theses would make the equipment for deductions cumbersome. The above catalog is what may be regarded as a compromise between these two evils.

In legal reasoning, dilemmata play a considerable practical role. They are widely employed in polemics, in which lawyers, too, often participate. Because of their rather complex structure, they lend themselves to abuse: invalid arguments here are not easy to detect for those not sufficiently trained in logic. The main types of dilemmata in propositional calculus are the following:

| | *Name* | *Abbreviation* | *Formula* |
|---|---|---|---|
| 1. | Simple Constructive Dilemma | S.C.D. | $CKKCpqCrqAprq$<br>$CKKCpqCrq\bar{E}prq$ |
| 2. | Simple Destructive Dilemma | S.D.D. | $CKKCpqCprAqrp$<br>$CKKCpqCpr\bar{E}\bar{q}\bar{r}\bar{p}$ |
| 3. | Complex Constructive Dilemma | C.D.D. | $CKKCpqCrsAprAqs$<br>$CKKCpqCrs\bar{E}prAqs$ |
| 4. | Complex Destructive Dilemma | C.D.D. | $CKKCpqCrsA\bar{q}\bar{s}A\bar{p}\bar{r}$<br>$CKKCpqCrs\bar{E}\bar{q}\bar{s}A\bar{p}\bar{r}$ |

The further three theses of propositional calculus also require special attention, because they lead to results which may surprise laymen in logic:

| | *Name* | *Abbreviation* | *Formula* |
|---|---|---|---|
| 1. | *Ex Falso Quodlibet* | F.Q. | $CKp\bar{p}q$ |
| | *Ex Quolibet Verum* | Q.V. | $CpAq\bar{q}$ |
| | *Consequentia Mirabilis* | C.M. | $CC\bar{p}pp$ |

## II. A SYSTEM OF PREDICATIONAL CALCULUS

### 1. *Preliminary Considerations about Predicational Calculus*

The thought-formations to which propositional calculus applies are indicatives as unanalyzed units of thought. There are logical arguments whose soundness ostensibly depends on the internal structure of the indicatives involved, for example:

All explosives are dangerous substances
Dynamite is an explosive

---

Dynamite is a dangerous substance

Paul is older than Dick
Dick is older than John

---

Paul is older than John

Neither of these arguments proves to be sound as a propositional inference considering that the propositional form of both is $CKpqr$. Nevertheless both appear to lead to logically valid conclusions warranted by common elements in their respective premisses. To actualize the inferential possibilities lying in these two kinds of argument, a special analysis of the content of their premisses is required and, correspondingly, appropriate symbolic devices. The requisite logical equipment is supplied by predicational calculus. For this calculus, it is preferable to employ the word "predicational" rather than "predicate" (which is ordinarily used), above all because it is the former that refers to those thought-formations with which the calculus is primarily concerned.

A predication is an indicative articulated into its logically significant elements. These elements are the *predicator* and at least one *hypotact*. The word "predicator" is preferable to the word "predicate" (still, regrettably, often used in standard works on modern logic), because in modern logic "predicate" does not mean the same concept as in traditional logic and because the rather different meaning which "predicate" has in grammar may be a source of confusion in any event. The word "hypotact" is a neologism introduced here to replace the ambiguous word "argument", which is frequently used for naming the logical entities governed by predicators. The predicators belong to the category of logical functors whereas the hypotacts belong to the category of logical fungenda. In predicational expressions there is no symbol for the copula, which would link a predicator with its hypotact or hypotacts. In the symbolic expression of a predication, the contiguity of a predicator and its hypotact or hypotacts expresses that the former governs the latter. The relevant circumstance can also be so viewed that the notion of predicator implies its assignment to its hypotact or hypotacts.

A characteristic feature of certain predications is the quantification of hypotacts, by which the extent is indicated to which hypotacts are governed by their predicators. It is performed by means of *quantors*, which are a kind of functor. The principles of quantification constitute the core of predicational calculus. Their main significance lies in giving rise to special predicational inferences.

Predicational calculus receives its logical operators from propositional calculus. These operators are here functors for predications, which as wholes are fungenda in relation to these functors. Just as propositions, predications can be linked with each other, under the relevant rules of formation, by means of junctors ( C , A , etc. ). The negator operates here on predications or their compounds. For negating a predication, the negator is placed on top of the predicator. The requirements of axiomatization stated in ch.I, s.1 apply also to predicational calculus. Here, too, the distinction between the object- and the meta-language of logic is to be noted.

Predications are either monadic or polyadic; the former govern only one hypotact, the latter two or more of them. Polyadic predications may be called "relations" and their predicators "relators". Regrettably, the word "relation" is often used for what should be called "relator". In the following, mainly those relations are considered whose relators govern two hypotacts.

In order to preserve the unity of the present system of notation, no brackets will be employed in predicational calculus, too. According to the relevant rules of formation, predicators occur only on the left hand side of the hypotacts they govern. Such a placement imposes a linguistic strain on the translations of predicational formulae into ordinary language. Linguistically, it would be more natural to place predicators after their hypotacts in monadic predications and between their hypotacts in dyadic predications. However, in case of triadic, tetradic, etc. predications, the placement of predicators is not linguistically fixed. Moreover, the following of patterns of ordinary language in logical expressions would produce inelegant and unwieldy formulae; it would make it necessary to employ brackets or their substitutes.

Predicational calculus provides formulae capable or expressing rigorously the principles of traditional logic. Since it does not share the assumptions of the latter, some forms of predicational inference are rather different from the forms of inference of Aristotelian syllogistics. Thus the immediate inferences under the principle of subalternation or under the principle of conversion by limitation appear in predicational calculus as mediate inferences having two premisses (instead of one premiss) and *Modus Darapti* as well as *Modus Felapton* appear as "ultrasyllogistic" inferences having three (instead of two) premisses.

The signs employed in the present system of predicational calculus are the following:

(1) The same signs as in propositional calculus for the operators ( $^{-}$ , C , K , etc. ).
(2) Small italics of ordinary size (e.g. *x* , *v* , *a* ), which stand for hypotact variables. They symbolize, within a

hypotact category, any hypotact whatsoever.

(3) Small italics of reduced size (e.g. $n$ , $a$ ), which stand for hypotact instances. They symbolize, within a hypotact category, determinate hypotacts.

(4) Capital italics of ordinary size (e.g. $F$ , $R$ ), which stand for predicator variables. They symbolize, within a predicator category, any predicator whatsoever.

(5) Capital italics of reduced size (e.g. $H$ , $O$ ), which stand for predicator instances. They symbolize, within a predicator category, determinate predicators.

(6) A cap ( $\wedge$ ) and a wedge ( $\vee$ ), which stand for quantification coefficients (viz. for the universalizer coefficient and for the particularizer coefficient respectively).

As in propositional calculus, subscripts will be employed in predicational expressions, too. On some occasions, also superscripts will be employed.

## 2. *The Rules of Formation of Predicational Calculus*

The rules of formation of predicational calculus serve for determining whether a symbolic expression represents an admissible unit in this calculus. There are some signs which belong to it, but alone do not constitute a predicational formula. A symbolic expression that satisfies the conditions laid down in the relevant rules constitutes a *well-formed predicational formula* , here abbreviated as "WFEF".

For its complete (as distinguished from its abbreviated ) notation, the rules of formation of the present system of predicational calculus are:

An expression is a WFEF if it is exactly either

(1) a capital italic, with or without a superscript, immediately followed by a small italic or small italics with or without a subscript; or

(2) any such expression with any number of bars on top of the capital letter; or

(3) two WFEFs immediately preceded by a junctor either without a bar or any number of bars on its top; or

(4) a WFEF immediately preceded by a quantor either without a bar or any number of bars on its top.

As subscripts, minuscle arabic numbers are employed; as superscripts, any convenient sign is employed. In the abbreviated notation, small italics are suppressed.

Examples of WFEFs:

Under Rule (1): $Fx$ , $Rx_1yx_2$ , $R'xa$

Under Rule (2): $\bar{F}x$ , $\bar{\bar{R}}m_1m_2n$ , $\bar{\bar{\bar{S}}}^cxyzx_1$

Under Rule (3): $C\ Fx\ Gx$ , $\bar{E}\ \bar{R}ae\ \bar{\bar{S}}xy$ , $\bar{\bar{A}}\ Fx\ K\ \bar{G}y\ Rax_1x_2$

Under Rule (4): $\underset{x}{\wedge}Fx$ , $\underset{x}{\bar{\bar{\vee}}}C\ Fx\ \bar{G}x$ , $\underset{xy}{\bar{\wedge}\vee}K\ Rxy\ \bar{D}\ F^mx\ E\ F^ny\ \bar{\bar{A}}\ Gy\ \underset{y}{\bar{\vee}}\bar{S}xya$

In order to ascertain whether an expression is a WFEF,

(1) ignore first the quantors and treat every elementary predicational formula as if it were an elementary propositional formula, then apply to them the instructions stated for the testing whether a formula is a WFOF;

(2) inspect whether the expression satisfies Rule (4) as stated above at every relevant point of the formula.

In the present system, the expressions belonging to it are employed as follows:

(1) A small italic from the end of the alphabet (viz. $x$ , $y$ , $z$ ) with or without a subscript stands for a *synopic hypotact with unlimited range of application*, which means that it represents any entity whatsoever within an unspecified universe of discourse. Accordingly, $x$ may be read as "whatever it may be". Any italic consonant other than $x$ and $z$ stands for a *synopic hypotact with limited range of application* , which means that it represents any entity whatsoever within a specified universe of discourse (e.g. a man, a town, a criminal). The limitation of the range of application of synopic hypotacts is not indispensable for the construction of predicational calculus. However, it proves expedient for some practical purposes, because it can yield shorter formulae. A small italic vowel other than $y$ stands for *stigmic hypotact* , which means an individual constant (e.g. Oliver Wendell Holmes, the City of New York).

(2) A capital italic of ordinary size stands for a *predicator variable*, that is, for any predicator whatsoever. A capital italic of reduced size stands for a *predicator instance*, that is, for a determinate predicator. In dealing with the theoretical foundations of predicational calculus, $F$ , $G$ , and $H$ are used for monadic and $R$ , $S$ , and $T$ for polyadic predications (to follow established practice). In practical applications of legal logic, this preference is supplanted by the consideration of supplying convenient mnemonic labels for key thoughts expressed in ordinary language.

(3) The quantification coefficients " $\wedge$ " and " $\vee$ " can be rendered as "every" and "some" respectively. Both can occur only on top of synopic hypotacts. Thus combined, the former is a component of U-quantor (which may also be called "universalizer"), whereas the latter is a component of a P-quantor (which may also be called "particularizer"). In the present system, only hypotacts are quantified.

The WFEFs which contain only hypotacts together with predicators that are not negated and not quantified are *elementary predicational formulae* . The WFEFs containing only one operator, likewise those quantified by a quantor that is not negated are *simple compound predicational formulae*. All other WFEFs are *complex compound predicational formulae* .

The quantor " $\underset{x}{\wedge}$ " can be rendered as "For every $x$: ...", whereas the quantor " $\underset{x}{\vee}$ " can be rendered as "For some $x$: ...". The sign configuration " $\underset{x\,y}{\wedge\vee}$ " can be rendered as "For every $x$ and for some $y$: ...". A quantor alone is not a WFEF, but forms a WFEF together with the formula which it governs. *The (synopic) hypotacts that are contained in a quantor must have correspondents in the WFEF following it and vice versa.* The range of application of a quantor is the WFEF which immediately follows it. Occurrence of a different quantor breaks the application of the previous quantor insofar that it contains the same hypotact as the preceding quantor does. Double quantifications, that is, applications of a quantor to a formula already quantified by the same quantor, are not admitted in the present system.

An unquantified (synopic) hypotact is a *free variable*, viz. a *free hypotact*; a formula which contains it is an *open formula*. A quantified (synopic) hypotact is a *bound variable*, viz. a *bound hypotact*; a formula which contains no free variable is a *closed formula*. Also those formulae which contain either only stigmic hypotacts or these together with bound hypotacts are closed formulae. Open formulae stand for incompletely expressed thoughts. They may be useful as logical expressions of vagueness of thought. Logical operations which depend on truth values can find only limited application with open formulae.

It is to be noted that when a negator occurs on top of a functor, the entire formula to which the functor applies is thereby negated. Thus a bar on top of a quantor negates the whole formula which the quantor governs.

In the symbolic language of logic, also those formulae are admissible which contain both WFOFs and WFEFs. An example of such mixed and yet well-formed formulae is the following: $C \underset{\chi}{\Diamond}\bar{E}\ Fx\ Gx\ A\ p\ K \underset{\chi}{\vee} Hx\ q$ .

For those predicational formulae in which only one synopic hypotact occurs, an abbreviated notation can be employed by simply omitting it, provided that it is consistently done in the same context. For example, instead of writing $Fx$ , $F$ alone can be written, and instead of writing $\underset{\chi}{\Diamond}K\ Fx\ \bar{G}x$ , $\wedge K\ F\ \bar{G}$ can be written. In the abbreviated notation, only the symbolic expression of thought is shortened, not the thought itself that is thereby expressed. In spelling out an abbreviated formula in ordinary language, it is necessary to mention the omitted synopic hypotacts.

### 3. *Construction of a System of Predicational Calculus*

In constructing the present system of predicational calculus, it is presumed that all definitions, axioms, rules of transformation, and theorems of propositional calculus hold for the predications (WFEFs). In the following exposition of the system, first its principles are stated in connection with formulae expressing monadic predications and then additional principles are stated which apply to formulae expressing dyadic predications:

*Definitions:* Df.U.: $\bigwedge_{x} Fx \leftrightarrow - - - K\ Fa_1\ Fa_2 \ldots$

Df.P.: $\bigvee_{x} Fx \leftrightarrow - - - A\ Fa_1\ Fa_2 \ldots$

The hyphens ( - - - ) in the definiens indicate that the formulae can be indefinitely extended by adding the relevant junctors in the front; the leaders ( . . . ) in the definiens indicate that the formulae can be indefinitely extended by adding correspondigly the predications $Fa_3$, $Fa_4$, etc. in the end. The first definition has the following corollary:

Cr.U.: $\bigwedge_{x} Fx \rightarrow K\ Fa_1\ Fa_2$ ,

where the metalogical sign "$\rightarrow$" indicates that the formula on its right hand side can be inferred from the formula on its left hand side.

According to the above definitions, predicational calculus can be reduced to propositional calculus in *finite* universes of discourse. If predicational calculus relates also to infinite universes of discourse, *rules of predicational derivation* have to be postulated. In the application of these rules it is assumed that any (synopic) hypotact quantified by the P-quantor has at least one instance of application. The so-called existential import here involved does not require an "ontological commitment" of predicational logic in the sense that the application instance in question must be something that is real. It can belong to the real world, but also to the world of imagination: it can be what is conceivable, but also what is inconceivable as a matter of fact.

For an easier formulation of the rules of predicational derivation, the following expressions are used:

(1) "equipredicative formula" to mean a predication which has exactly the same predicator as another predication;

(2) "universalized formula" to mean a predication quantified by the U-quantor and not governed by an operator;

(3) "particularized formula" to mean a predication quantified by the P-quantor and not governed by an operator;

(4) "singular formula" to mean a predication containing at least one stigmic hypotact;

(5) "corresponding formula" to mean a predication none of whose hypotacts is excluded from the application range of its counterpart in another formula and in which a stigmic hypotact occurs in place of a synopic hypotact in the latter or vice versa.

The application of these rules can take place only if the relevant universe of discourse can be regarded as not being empty. This means in particular that the universalized formulae must not have for *all* their application instances that which does not exist in the pertinent universe of discourse. *The application of a rule must always be consistent.*

*Rules of Derivation:*

Universal Stigmication (U.T.): From any universalized formula it is permissible to derive any corresponding equipredicative formula.

For example, from $\underset{\chi}{\wedge}Fx$ it is permissible to derive $Fa$; from $\underset{\chi}{\wedge}K\ Fx\ Ga$ it is permissible to derive $K\ Fa\ Ga$. Note, however, that from $\underset{\chi}{\wedge}K\ Fx\ Gx$ it is not permissible to derive $K\ Fa\ Gx$.

Particular Stigmication (P.T.): From any particularized formula it is permissible to derive one corresponding equipredicative formula, provided that the stigmic hypotact in it does occur previously in the given derivation context.

For example, (with the above proviso) from $\underset{\chi}{\vee}Fx$ it is permissible to derive $Fa$, whereas from $\underset{\chi}{\vee}K\ Fx\ Ga$ it is not permissible to derive $K\ Fa\ Ga$. Note that from $\underset{\chi}{\vee}K\ Fx\ Gx$ it is not permissible to derive $K\ Fa\ Gx$.

Particular Synopication (P.S.): From any singular formula it is permissible to derive any corresponding equipredicative particularized formula.

For example, from $Fa$ it is permissible to derive $\bigvee_x Fx$. Note that if the relevant formula has, for instance, the form $\bigvee_x K\ Fx\ Ga$, it is not permissible to derive $\bigvee_x K\ Fx\ Gx$ ; a permissible derivation here is $\bigvee_x \bigvee_y K\ Fx\ Gy$ .

Universal Synopication (U.Y.): From any singular formula it is permissible to derive a corresponding equipredicative universalized formula, provided that in the singular formula the hypotact to be replaced is one that was derived under U.T. in the given derivation context.

For example, (with the above proviso) from $Fa$ it is permissible to derive $\bigwedge_x Fx$. Note that if $Fa$ was derived from $\bigwedge_y Fy$ under P.T. previously, it is not permissible to derive from it $\bigwedge_x Fx$ under U.Y., that from $K\ Fa\ Ga$ it is not permissible to derive $\bigwedge_x K\ Fx\ Ga$, and from $\bigwedge_x K\ Fx\ Ga$ it is not permissible to derive $\bigwedge_x \bigwedge_x K\ Fx\ Gx$ .

In the above sets of examples, any junctor could have been used instead of $K$.

The above rules apply also to polyadic predications. Thus $Rae$ can be derived from $\bigwedge_x \bigwedge_y Rxy$ under U.T. and $\bigvee_x \bigvee_y Sxey$ can be derived from $Saeo$ under P.Y. Not permissible are, for example, $\bigwedge_x Rxa$ from $Raa$ (under U.Y.), $\bigwedge_x \bigvee_x Rxa$ from $\bigvee_x Rxa$ (under U.Y.), and $\bigvee_x Rxx$ from $\bigvee_x Rxa$ (under P.Y.).

Relational formulae admit further inferential possibilities on the basis of certain logically significant properties of their relators. These properties appear from relational formulae as the following, which present some important types of dyadic relations. The relational hypotacts are usually called "terms". They may also be called "relata" (to have a terminological unity with "relator" and "relation").

*Properties of Dyadic Relators:*

| | |
|---|---|
| (1) Symmetry (Sym.) | $\bigwedge_x \bigwedge_y E\ Rxy\ Ryx$ |
| (2) Asymmetry (Asym.) | $\bigwedge_x \bigwedge_y C\ Rxy\ \bar{R}yx$ |
| (3) Parasymmetry (P.sym.) | $\bar{A}\ \bigwedge_x \bigwedge_y E\ Rxy\ Ryx\ \bigwedge_x \bigwedge_y C\ Rxy\ \bar{R}yx$ |
| (4) Non-symmetry (N.-sym.) | $\bigvee_x \bigvee_y \bar{E}\ Rxy\ Ryx$ |
| (5) Non-asymmetry (N.-asym.) | $\bigvee_x \bigvee_y \bar{C}\ Rxy\ \bar{R}yx$ |
| (6) Non-parasymmetry (N.-p.sym.) | $A\ \bigwedge_x \bigwedge_y E\ Rxy\ Ryx\ \bigwedge_x \bigwedge_y C\ Rxy\ \bar{R}yx$ |

(7) Reflexivity (Refl.) $\bigwedge_{x} Rxx$

(8) Irreflexivity (Irrefl.) $\bigwedge_{x} \bar{R}xx$

(9) Parareflexivity (P-refl.) $\bar{A} \bigwedge_{x} Rxx \bigwedge_{x} \bar{R}xx$

(10) Conversity (Conv.) $\bigwedge_{x}\bigwedge_{y} E\ Rxy\ Syx$

(11) Inconversity (Inconv.) $\bigwedge_{x}\bigwedge_{y} C\ Rxy\ \bar{S}yx$

(12) Paraconversity (P.conv.) $\bar{A} \bigwedge_{x}\bigwedge_{y} E\ Rxy\ Syx \bigwedge_{x}\bigwedge_{y} C\ Rxy\ \bar{S}yx$

(13) Transitivity (Trans.) $\bigwedge_{x}\bigwedge_{y}\bigwedge_{z} C\ K\ Rxy\ Ryz\ Rxz$

(14) Intransitivity (Intrans.) $\bigwedge_{x}\bigwedge_{y}\bigwedge_{z} C\ K\ Rxy\ Rzy\ \bar{R}xz$

(15) Paratransitivity (P.trans.) $\bar{A} \bigwedge_{x}\bigwedge_{y}\bigwedge_{z} C\ K\ Rxy\ Ryz\ Rxz$ -
$\bigwedge_{x}\bigwedge_{y}\bigwedge_{z} C\ K\ Rxy\ Ryz\ \bar{R}xz$

There are also non-reflexive, non-irreflexive, non-para-reflexive, non-conversive, etc. relations. The properties of their relators would appear from the formulae in which the corresponding positive relations are negated.

The derivation of the theorems of predicational calculus follows the same pattern as the derivation of the theorems of propositional calculus. Additional principles of predicational calculus appear here among the reasons for derivational steps. In the derivation of those theorems involving only one synopic hypotact, abbreviated notation may be employed. This is not feasible where relational formulae are involved.

Th.1:

| | | |
|---|---|---|
| 1. | $\wedge F$ | /- $C \wedge F \vee F$ |
| 2. | $Fa$ | 1, U.T. |
| 3. | $\vee F$ | 2, P.Y. |
| 4. | $C \wedge F \vee F$ | 1,3, P.D.F. |

Th.2:

| | | |
|---|---|---|
| 1. | $\bar{\wedge} F$ | /- $C \bar{\wedge} F \vee \bar{F}$ |
| 2. | $\bar{K}\ \bar{F}a_1\ \bar{F}a_2$ | 1, Cr.U., R.R. |
| 3. | $A\ \bar{F}a_1\ \bar{F}a_2$ | 2, Dual. |
| 4. | $- - - A\ \bar{F}a_1\ \bar{F}a_2 \ldots$ | 3, Add. |

5. $\vee\bar{F}$ 4, Df.P.

6. $C\ \bar{\wedge}F\ \vee\bar{F}$ 1,5, P.D.F.

Th.3:

1. $\wedge C\ F\ G$

2. $\vee K\ H\ F$ /- $C\ K\ \wedge C\ F\ G\ \vee K\ H\ F\ \vee K\ H\ G$

3. $K\ Ha\ Fa$ 2, P.T.

4. $C\ Fa\ Ga$ 1, U.T.

5. $Ha$ 3, C.E.

6. $Fa$ 3, C.E.

7. $Ga$ 4,6, R.D.

8. $K\ Ha\ Ga$ 5,7, R.C.

9. $\vee K\ H\ G$ 8, P.Y.

10. $K\ \wedge C\ F\ G\ \vee K\ H\ F$ 1,2, R.C.

11. $C\ K\ \wedge C\ F\ G\ \vee K\ H\ F\ \vee K\ H\ G$ 10,9, P.D.F.

In the following derivation, the properties of the relator involved are indicated in the ordinary brackets. The bracketed expression constitutes the only premiss of the inference. The derived theorem is to the effect that any relation whose relator has the properties of transitivity and irreflexivity is also a relation whose relator has the property of asymmetry.

Th.4:

( 1. $R$ - Trans.,Irrefl. ) /- $\bigwedge_{xy} C\ Rxy\ \overline{Ryx}$

2. $\bigwedge_{xy} C\ K\ Rxy\ Ryx\ Rxx$ 1, Trans.

3. $C\ K\ Rae\ Rea\ Raa$ 2, U.T.

4. $\bigwedge_{x} \overline{Rxx}$ 1, Irrefl.

5. $\overline{Raa}$ 4, U.T.

6. $\bar{K}\ Rae\ Rea$ 3,5, M.T.

7. $A\ \overline{Rae}\ \overline{Rea}$ 6, Dual., D.N.

| | | |
|---|---|---|
| 8. | $C\ Rae\ \bar{R}ea$ | 7, Dual., D.N. |
| 9. | $\bigwedge_{xy} C\ Rxy\ \bar{R}yx$ | 8, U.Y. |

## 4. *A Catalog of Theorems of Predicational Calculus*

All theorems of this catalog are expressed in abbreviated notation. First those are listed which are particularly useful for deductions. The other theorems are included for showing a way to express forms of inference of traditional logic by means of modern logic. Those forms can conveniently be expressed also by the instrumentality of extensional calculus, but this method has no particular advantage over the method of predicational calculus.

Quantification Theorems

| | *Name* | *Abbreviation* | *Formula* |
|---|---|---|---|
| 1. | Universalizer Negation | U.N. | $E\ \overline{\wedge}F\ \vee\overline{F}$ |
| 2. | Particularizer Negation | P.N. | $E\ \overline{\vee}F\ \wedge\overline{F}$ |
| 3. | Quantor Subordination | Q.S. | $C\ \wedge F\ \vee F$ |
| 4. | Quantor Location | Q.L. | $E\ \wedge K\ F\ G\ K\ \wedge F\ \wedge G$<br>$E\ \vee A\ F\ G\ A\ \vee F\ \vee G$<br>$C\ \wedge C\ F\ G\ C\ \wedge F\ \wedge G$<br>$C\ \vee K\ F\ G\ K\ \vee F\ \vee G$<br>$C\ \wedge E\ F\ G\ E\ \wedge F\ \wedge G$<br>$C\ A\ \wedge F\ \wedge G\ \wedge A\ F\ G$ |

Forms of Inference of Traditional Logic

| | *Name* | *Abbreviation* | *Formula* |
|---|---|---|---|
| | **Syllogistic Theorems** | | |
| 1. | *Modus Ponendo Ponens* | M.P.P. | $C\ K\ \wedge C\ F\ G\ \vee F\ \vee G$ |
| 2. | *Modus Tollendo Tollens* | M.T.T. | $C\ K\ \wedge C\ F\ G\ \vee\overline{G}\ \vee\overline{F}$ |
| 3. | *Modus Ponendo Tollens* | M.P.T. | $C\ K\ \wedge\overline{E}\ F\ G\ \vee F\ \vee\overline{G}$<br>$C\ K\ \wedge\overline{E}\ F\ G\ \vee G\ \vee\overline{F}$ |
| 4. | *Modus Tollendo Ponens* | M.T.P. | $C\ K\ \wedge A\ F\ G\ \vee\overline{F}\ \vee G$<br>$C\ K\ \wedge A\ F\ G\ \vee\overline{G}\ \vee F$ |

| | | | |
|---|---|---|---|
| | *Modus Tollendo Ponens* | | $C\,K\,\wedge\bar{E}\,F\,G\,\vee\bar{F}\,\vee G$ |
| | | | $C\,K\,\wedge\bar{E}\,F\,G\,\vee\bar{G}\,\vee F$ |
| 5. | *Modus Barbara* | Barb. | $C\,K\,\wedge C\,F\,G\,\wedge C\,H\,F\,\wedge C\,H\,G$ |
| 6. | *Modus Celarent* | Cel. | $C\,K\,\wedge C\,F\,\bar{G}\,\wedge C\,H\,F\,\wedge C\,H\,\bar{G}$ |
| 7. | *Modus Darii* | Darii | $C\,K\,\wedge C\,F\,G\,\vee K\,H\,F\,\vee K\,H\,G$ |
| 8. | *Modus Ferio* | Ferio | $C\,K\,\wedge C\,F\,\bar{G}\,\vee K\,H\,F\,\vee K\,H\,\bar{G}$ |
| 9. | *Modus Cesare* | Ces. | $C\,K\,\wedge C\,F\,\bar{G}\,\wedge C\,H\,G\,\wedge C\,H\,\bar{F}$ |
| 10. | *Modus Camestres* | Cames. | $C\,K\,\wedge C\,F\,G\,\wedge C\,H\,\bar{G}\,\wedge C\,H\,\bar{F}$ |
| 11. | *Modus Festino* | Fest. | $C\,K\,\wedge C\,F\,\bar{G}\,\vee K\,H\,G\,\vee K\,H\,\bar{F}$ |
| 12. | *Modus Baroco* | Baro. | $C\,K\,\wedge C\,F\,G\,\vee K\,H\,\bar{G}\,\vee K\,H\,\bar{F}$ |
| 13. | *Modus Disamis* | Dis. | $C\,K\,\vee K\,F\,G\,\wedge C\,F\,H\,\vee K\,H\,G$ |
| 14. | *Modus Datisi* | Dat. | $C\,K\,\wedge C\,F\,G\,\vee K\,F\,H\,\vee K\,H\,G$ |
| 15. | *Modus Bocardo* | Boc. | $C\,K\,\vee K\,F\,\bar{G}\,\wedge C\,F\,H\,\vee K\,H\,\bar{G}$ |
| 16. | *Modus Ferison* | Feris. | $C\,K\,\wedge C\,F\,\bar{G}\,\vee K\,F\,H\,\vee K\,H\,\bar{G}$ |
| 17. | *Modus Camenes* | Camen. | $C\,K\,\wedge C\,F\,G\,\wedge C\,G\,\bar{H}\,\wedge C\,H\,\bar{F}$ |
| 18. | *Modus Dimaris* | Dim. | $C\,K\,\vee K\,F\,G\,\wedge C\,G\,H\,\vee K\,H\,F$ |
| 19. | *Modus Fresison* | Fre. | $C\,K\,\wedge C\,F\,\bar{G}\,\vee K\,G\,H\,\vee K\,H\,\bar{F}$ |

Ultrasyllogistic Theorems

| | | | |
|---|---|---|---|
| 1. | *Modus Darapti* | Dara. | $C\,K\,K\,\wedge C\,F\,G\,\vee F\,\wedge C\,F\,H\,\vee K\,H\,G$ |
| 2. | *Modus Felapton* | Fel. | $C\,K\,K\,\wedge C\,F\,\bar{G}\,\vee F\,\wedge C\,F\,H\,\vee K\,H\,\bar{G}$ |
| 3. | *Modus Bramantip* | Bram. | $C\,K\,K\,\wedge C\,F\,G\,\vee F\,\wedge C\,G\,H\,\vee K\,H\,F$ |
| 4. | *Modus Fesapo* | Fesa. | $C\,K\,K\,\wedge C\,F\,\bar{G}\,\vee G\,\wedge C\,G\,H\,\vee K\,H\,\bar{F}$ |

## III. Current Methods for Proving Logical Validity and Solidity

### 1. *Preliminary Considerations about Logical Proofs*

The equipment of propositional and predicational calculi supplied in the previous chapters can be employed to prove whether the claimed conclusions of arguments logically follow from the provided premisses, that is, whether these conclusions are *logically valid*. The logical frame of the corresponding inferences is a tautologous subjunction in which the derivation base constitutes the antecedent and the conclusion constitutes the consequent.

By applying relevant logical principles to posited antecedents of such subjunctions, their consequents can be derived. However, this may not be a fully satisfactory outcome of a reasoning. Under the theorem *Ex Falso Quodlibet* formally valid conclusions can be derived from logically inconsistent premisses, that is, from premisses which are dyslogous (i.e. self-contradictory) or whose conjunction is dyslogous (i.e. whose conjuncts are contradictory to each other). Such valid conclusions are precarious because under the same theorem also their negations would be valid conclusions as a matter of logic. To eliminate the intellectual license which is thus opened, it is necessary to add - as a requirement for practical applications of logic - that logical conclusions must not rest on a dyslogous derivation base. This requirement relates to what may be called "*logical solidity*". Particularly in legal applications of logic it is expected that logical conclusions be both *valid* and *solid*.

Logical inference is a kind of logical argument. The word "argument" is used in this book to mean above all that reasoning which seeks to establish that the conclusion claimed for an inference is not only logically valid but also logically solid. The inferences in which logically valid conclusions are drawn from dyslogous derivation bases may be theoretically interesting and useful. However, they are not arguments of any obvious merit in the legal universe of discourse.

The deductive instrumentarium supplied above is employed in the present chapter to construct ordinary deductive proofs, usually divided into direct, indirect, and conditional proofs. These serve for establishing the validity of conclusions in the areas of propositional and predicational calculi. However, they are not apt for demonstrating the invalidity of what may be claimed as conclusions of inferences. The fact that a reasoner does not succeed in providing a proof for a claimed conclusion does not warrant the invalidity of this conclusion. It may happen that he has lacked insight, ingenuity, patience, or time for achieving the purported proof, which is still available. On some occasions, the validity of the negation of a claimed conclusion can be proved, whereas the attempts to prove the validity of this conclusion remain unavailing. This constitutes a reason to suspect, but not a sufficient reason to believe, that the conclusion is invalid. There is further the possibility that both a formula and its negation are valid conclusions of an inference. In this case both conclusions must be insolid, because they must rest on a dyslogous derivation base. This means that the inference in the given case is unsound in any event; in other words, it is not a rational argument. To refute a logical inference as a rational argument may be all that is required for practical purposes.

There are logical methods by which it is possible to decide whether a claimed conclusion is *either* valid *or* invalid. These methods are called "*decision-procedures*". The ordinary deductive proofs do not constitute decision-procedures. By these procedures it is possible to determine in all cases whether a claimed conclusion is *either* solid *or* insolid, too. The existence and great utility of decision-procedures does not render the ordinary deductive proof methods useless. On many occasions they are the simplest and the most efficient ways of establishing the validity of conclusions. In order to make the best use of them, ingenuity and insight are often required. Thus in practising their application, these felicities of the mind are cultivated.

A standard decision-procedure of propositional calculus, which has a limited application also in predicational calculus, is the full tabular method. This method provides the basis for another useful decision-procedure, the so-called short-cut tabular method. Both methods proceed from the ascription of the values "true" and "false" to indicative formulae. The tabular method constitutes an alternative foundation of propositional calculus aside from axiomatic method. As compared with the latter, it is most expedient for ascertaining whether a formula represents a logical thesis where only a few propositional variables are involved. However, the full tabular method proves to be cumbrous even where more than three propositional variables occur in the formulae to be tested. The short-cut tabular method can be very efficient even where the formulae contain many variables; but it proves to be cumbrous, too, in connection witn certain formulae. Logicians have looked for further decision-procedures which would be more efficient than the tabular method. Such a decision procedure is the counter-formula method, to which a separate chapter will be devoted in this book.

## 2. *The Methods of Direct, Indirect, and Conditional Proof*

The three methods of ordinary deductive proof: those of direct, indirect, and conditional proof, lead to the same result but in different ways, of which one may be more efficient than the others in a given case. None of them provides a logical decision-procedure - they are designed to demonstrate only the validity of arguments. But by extending their deductive equipment, they can be developed into decision-procedures. Thus the indirect proof method can be developed into the counter-formula method.

Here is a typical deductive proof:

| | | |
|---|---|---|
| 1. | $C A p q K r s$ | |
| 2. | $A p \bar{s}$ | |
| 3. | $\bar{p}$ | /,', $\underline{\bar{q}}$ |
| 4. | $\bar{s}$ | 2,3, A.E. |
| 5. | $A \bar{s} \bar{r}$ | 4, Add. |
| 6. | $A \bar{r} \bar{s}$ | 5, Comm. |
| 7. | $\bar{K} r s$ | 6, Dual., D.N. |
| 8. | $\bar{A} p q$ | 1,7, M.T. |
| 9. | $K \bar{p} \bar{q}$ | 8, Dual., D.N. |
| 10. | $\bar{q}$ | 9, C.E. |

In the above schema, which represents a *direct proof*, the premisses of the inference are set down in the derivation column as Entries 1 to 3. The order in which the premisses occur is immaterial. On occasion, there may be only one premiss. Where there are several premisses, they are written on separate lines and numbered consecutively. The conclusion of the inference is written after the premisses and to the right of the last premiss. It is preceded by the sign " /,', ", which belongs to logical meta-language and which can be read as "therefore" or "consequently". The proof is written below the premisses. Each step of the proof is written on a separate line and the consecutive numbering continues from where the premisses end. A simple step is constituted by the application of a single logical thesis. A complex step is constituted by the application of several logical theses. An example of a complex step is Step 7, which was made by recourse to the theorems of Duality and Double Negation. Each step in the proof has to be justified by stating how it was obtained. This is done in the justification column, where to the right of the entry for the step to be justified the number of the entry in the proof is written on which the step rests and the abbreviated name of the relevant theorem.

In addition to the previously supplied deductive equipment, a further rule may be added as a measure of convenience:

Tautology Insertion (T.I.): Any tautologous formula can be inserted as an entry into any proof.

This rule, although dispensable, can be useful for rendering some proofs easier to perform. The following is an example of its application:

| | | |
|---|---|---|
| 1. | $C A K p q K p \bar{q} r$ | |
| 2. | $A p K s \bar{s}$ | /.'. $\underline{r}$ |
| 3. | $\bar{K} s \bar{s}$ | T.I. |
| 4. | $p$ | 2,3, A.E. |
| 5. | $A q \bar{q}$ | T.I. |
| 6. | $K p A q \bar{q}$ | 4,5, R.C. |
| 7. | $A K p q K p \bar{q}$ | 6, Distr. |
| 8. | $r$ | 1,7, M.P. |

The next example of direct proof contains formulae in which only monadic predications with a single synopic hypotact occur. Therefore abbreviated predicational notation can be employed here.

| | | |
|---|---|---|
| 1. | $\wedge C\ F\ G$ | |
| 2. | $\vee K\ H\ F$ | /.'. $\underline{\vee K\ H\ G}$ |
| 3. | $K\ Ha\ Fa$ | 2, P.T. |
| 4. | $Fa$ | 3, C.E. |
| 5. | $C\ Fa\ Ga$ | 1, U.T. |
| 6. | $Ga$ | 5,4, M.P. |
| 7. | $Ha$ | 3, C.E. |

8. $K\,Ha\,Ga$ 7,6, R.C.

9. $\vee K\,H\,G$ 8, P.Y.

In *indirect proof*, the negation of the formula representing the conclusion of an inference is inserted as an additional entry in the proof. If this insertion leads to a dyslogous formula in the course of the proof, the claimed conclusion is established as logically valid. For according to the theorem *Tertium non Datur* ( $\bar{E}\,p\,\bar{p}$ ), there is no other possibility but the affirmation of the claimed conclusion.

The entry that involves the insertion of the negation of the conclusion of an inference is the first step in indirect proof. Its abbreviated name is "N.C." ("Negation of Conclusion"). The final step in indirect proof is the entry which represents the claimed conclusion; it rests on the immediately preceding step, which produces the conjunction of a formula appearing in the proof procedure and the negation of this formula. The abbreviated name of the final step is "I.P." ("Indirect Proof").

Examples of Indirect Proof:

1. $C\,p\,q$
2. $C\,K\,p\,q\,r$
3. $C\,K\,\bar{p}\,\bar{r}\,\bar{s}$ /∴ $\underline{C\,s\,r}$
4. $\bar{C}\,s\,r$ N.C.
5. $\bar{A}\,\bar{s}\,r$ 4, Dual.
6. $K\,s\,\bar{r}$ 5, Dual., D.N.
7. $s$ 6, C.E.
8. $\bar{K}\,\bar{p}\,\bar{r}$ 3,7, M.T.
9. $C\,K\,q\,p\,r$ 2, Comm.
10. $C\,q\,C\,p\,r$ 9, Exp.
11. $C\,p\,C\,p\,r$ 1,10, H.S.
12. $C\,K\,p\,p\,r$ 11, Exp.

| | | |
|---|---|---|
| 13. | $C \bar{A} \bar{p} \bar{p} r$ | 12, Dual. |
| 14. | $C p r$ | 13, Aut., D.N. |
| 15. | $\bar{r}$ | 6, C.E. |
| 16. | $\bar{p}$ | 14,15, M.T. |
| 17. | $A p r$ | 8, Dual. |
| 18. | $r$ | 17,16, A.E. |
| 19. | $K \bar{r} r$ | 15,18, R.C. |
| 20. | $C s r$ | 19, I.P. |

In the following proof, abbreviated notation of predicational calculus can be employed again.

| | | |
|---|---|---|
| 1. | $\wedge C\ G\ F$ | |
| 2. | $\vee \bar{C}\ H\ F$ | /.'. $\underline{\vee \bar{C}\ H\ G}$ |
| 3. | $\overline{\vee} \bar{C}\ H\ G$ | N.C. |
| 4. | $\wedge C\ H\ G$ | 3, P.N., D.N. |
| 5. | $\bar{C}\ Ha\ Fa$ | 2, P.T. |
| 6. | $C\ Ha\ Ga$ | 4, U.T. |
| 7. | $C\ Ga\ Fa$ | 1, U.T. |
| 8. | $C\ Ha\ Fa$ | 6,7, H.S. |
| 9. | $K\ C\ Ha\ Fa\ \bar{C}\ Ha\ Fa$ | 8,5, R.C. |
| 10. | $\vee \bar{C}\ H\ G$ | 9, I.P. |

*Conditional proof* can be expedient for ascertaining the logical validity of a conclusion which has the form of subjunction or which can be transformed into this form. It finds application especially where the deductive equipment provided by a logical system is otherwise not sufficient for providing the required proof. The basic idea of conditional proof consists in the application of the theorem of Exportation ( $E C p C q r C K p q r$ ), according to which $C p C q r$ can be replaced with $C K p q r$ . If the former represents a valid conclusion of an inference, also a conclusion in the form of the latter must be valid.

The proof in question is so constructed that the antecedent of the subjunctive conclusion is inserted as an additional entry into the derivation column of the inference. This is indicated by "I.A.C." ("Insertion of the Antecedent of Conclusion") in the justification column. The goal of the proof is achieved when it has been possible to derive from the premisses of the inference extended by the antecedent of its conclusion the consequent of the conclusion.

To bring out clearly the conditional phase of the proof, a part-frame can be used, which encloses this phase. The first entry in the part-frame is the additional entry; the last entry is the conclusion of the conditional phase of the proof. The entry immediately below the closed frame is the conclusion of the whole proof itself in the subjunctive form of the conclusion. The abbreviation which appears for it in the justification column is "C.P." ("Conditional Proof"). When required, the conditional proof procedure can be applied several times in the same inference. In this case, a further part-frame (or part-frames) can be drawn within the already existing frame (or frames). The conclusion of the whole proof appears in the subjunctive form then immediately below the last frame.

If the original conclusion does not have the form of subjunction, it is necessary to transform it accordingly. The corresponding formula is written down immediately below the original conclusion and is indicated in brackets by the abbreviation "T.C." ("Transformed Conclusion").

Examples of Conditional Proof:

1. $A\bar{p}Cqr$
2. $A\bar{q}Crs$     /∴ $A\bar{p}A\bar{q}s$
   $CpCqs$ (T.C.)

| | | |
|---|---|---|
| 3. | $p$ | I.A.C. |
| 4. | $q$ | I.A.C. |
| 5. | $Cqr$ | 1,3, A.E. |
| 6. | $r$ | 5,4, M.P. |

7. C r s — 2,4, A.E.

8. s — 7,6, M.P.

9. C q s — 4-8, C.P.

10. C p C q s — 3-9, C.P.

The following example involves relations. The outcome of the proof here depends also on the properties which the dyadic relator occurring in them has. It is stipulated to be such that it is both symmetric and transitive. This is indicated in brackets after the premiss by the corresponding abbreviations.

1. $\bigwedge_x \bigwedge_y \bigwedge_z$ C A *Fx Gy* K *Rxy Rzy*

( 2. R - Sym.,Trans. ) /.'. C *Fa Rai*

3. C A *Fa Ge* K *Rae Rie* — 1, U.T.

4. *Fa* — I.A.C.

5. A *Fa Ge* — 4, Add.

6. K *Rae Rie* — 3,5, M.P.

7. K *Rae Rei* — 2,6, Sym.

8. *Rai* — 2,7, Trans.

9. C *Fa Rai* — 4-8, C.P.

### 3. *The Full Tabular Method*

The decision-procedure which the full tabular method provides requires the ascription of semantic quality signs (SQSs) signifying the logical values "true" or "false" (usually called "truth-values") to elementary indicative formulae; it also requires the construction of constellations of these signs characterizing compound formulae. In the following exposition, " + " is employed to signify "true" and " - " to signify "false".

In the present system, an elementary formula ( p , q , r, etc.) can have either minus or plus. The number of various SQS constellations characterizing the compound formulae depends on the number of the elementary formulae which these contain. The possible SQS distributions for two elementary formulae is $2^2$ ( = 4 ), for three such formulae $2^3$ ( = 8 ), for four such formulae $2^4$ ( = 16 ), etc. In order to present these distributions so that they can be easily surveyed and remembered, they are set out in *leading columns* . These may be placed in front of the relevant compound formula or each column may be placed under the relevant elementary formula. The following table presents the leading columns for one, two, three, and four elementary propositional formulae.

Table I:

| p | p q | p q r | p q r s |
|---|---|---|---|
| + | + + | + + + | + + + + |
| − | + − | + + − | + + + − |
| | − + | + − + | + + − + |
| | − − | + − − | + + − − |
| | | − + + | + − + + |
| | | − + − | + − + − |
| | | − − + | + − − + |
| | | − − − | + − − − |
| | | | − + + + |
| | | | − + + − |
| | | | − + − + |
| | | | − + − − |
| | | | − − + + |
| | | | − − + − |
| | | | − − − + |
| | | | − − − − |

In order to obtain the SQS distributions which would represent all their possible combinations, proceed according the following instructions:

(1) Halve the first column and place plus into the first half and minus into the second half of the column.

(2) If there is a second column, halve each half of the previous column and place plus into the first resulting half and minus into the second half of the column.

(3) If there are further columns, halve each group of the signs until the configuration plus-minus-plus-minus ... is reached.

The specific SQS constellation which characterizes each compound formula is determined by the distribution of the signs in the leading columns and by the operator or the operators occurring in the formula. For a compound formula consisting of a monadic operator and one elementary formula, there are four possible constellations. For a compound formula formed by a junctor and two elementary formulae, there are sixteen possible constellations. For the present purposes, only some of these possible constellations will be selected, namely those which are employed to characterize the simple compound WFOFs formed by " $^-$ ", " C ", " A ", " K ", " E ", " D ", " $\bar{C}$ ", " $\bar{A}$ ", " $\bar{K}$ ", " $\bar{E}$ ", and " $\bar{D}$ ".

Table II:

| p | $\bar{p}$ |
|---|---|
| + | - |
| - | + |

| pq | Cpq | Apq | Kpq | Epq | Dpq |
|---|---|---|---|---|---|
| + + | + | + | + | + | + |
| + - | - | + | - | - | + |
| - + | + | + | - | - | - |
| - - | + | - | - | + | + |

| pq | $\bar{C}$pq | $\bar{A}$pq | $\bar{K}$pq | $\bar{E}$pq | $\bar{D}$pq |
|---|---|---|---|---|---|
| + + | - | - | - | - | - |
| + - | + | - | + | + | - |
| - + | - | - | + | + | + |
| - - | - | + | + | - | - |

The above table expresses the following:

(1) For the negator, plus gives minus and minus gives plus.

(2) For the subjunctor, only plus and minus give plus.

(3) For the adjunctor, only two minuses give minus.

(4) For the conjunctor, only two pluses give plus.

(5) For the bijunctor, the same signs give plus and the different signs give minus.

(6) For the dejunctor, only minus and plus give minus.

(7) For the contrasubjunctor, only plus and minus give plus.

(8) For the contraadjunctor, only two minuses give plus.

(9) For the contrabijunctor, the same signs give minus and the different signs give plus.

(10) For the contradejunctor, only minus and plus give plus.

The same table shows that the SQS constellations characterizing contrasubjunction, contraadjunction, contraconjunction, contrabijunction, and contradejunction are exactly the reverse of those characterizing subjunction, adjunction, conjunction, bijunction, and dejunction. This is to be expected, because the negator on top of the junctors has the effect of converting plus into minus and minus into plus in the constellation characterizing any formula on which it operates.

To work out the ultimate SQS constellation characterizing a complex compound formula, it is convenient to place the leading columns under the relevant elementary formulae. This is done in the following table. The columns appropriate to the negated elementary formulae appear in the matrix with the SQS constellations which are the reverse of those of the corresponding unnegated formulae.

Table III:

| E | $\bar{C}$ | C | p | $\bar{q}$ | $\bar{K}$ | r | $\bar{p}$ | $\bar{E}$ | K | q | $\bar{r}$ | p |
|---|---|---|---|---|---|---|---|---|---|---|---|---|
| − | − | − | + | − | + | + | − | + | − | + | − | + |
| + | − | − | + | − | + | − | − | − | + | + | + | + |
| − | − | + | + | + | + | + | − | + | − | − | − | + |
| − | − | + | + | + | + | − | − | + | − | − | + | + |
| − | + | + | − | − | − | + | + | − | − | + | − | − |
| − | − | + | − | − | + | − | + | + | + | + | + | − |
| − | + | + | − | + | − | + | + | − | − | − | − | − |
| + | − | + | − | + | + | − | + | − | − | − | + | − |

To employ the above technique, proceed as follows:

(1) Place the appropriate leading columns under the relevant simple formulae.

(2) Work out the constellations of each junctor placing the appropriate signs under it.

(3) Continue this procedure until the first junctor of the whole formula is reached.

The result in the above table was achieved by working out the SQS constellations for each junctor (with or without a bar on its top), commencing with K on the right hand side and moving to the left until the first junctor ( E ) was reached.

If the ultimate SQS constellation of a compound formula contains only pluses, only minuses, or both signs, it is called a "*tautology*", a "*dyslogy*", and an "*amphilogy*" respectively. Tautologous formulae represent theses of propositional calculus and dyslogous formulae represent propositional self-contradictions. In the following table, some of the axioms and theorems of propositional calculus are expressed and it is proved that they constitute tautologies.

Table IV:

| C | p | A | p | q | | C | K | p | $\bar{p}$ | q |
|---|---|---|---|---|---|---|---|---|---|---|
| + | + | + | + | + | | + | - | + | - | + |
| + | + | + | + | - | | + | - | + | - | - |
| + | - | + | - | + | | + | - | - | + | + |
| + | - | - | - | - | | + | - | - | + | - |

| C | C | p | q | C | A | r | p | A | r | q | | C | K | C | p | q | C | q | r | C | p | r |
|---|---|---|---|---|---|---|---|---|---|---|---|---|---|---|---|---|---|---|---|---|---|---|
| + | + | + | + | + | + | + | + | + | + | + | | + | + | + | + | + | + | + | + | + | + | + |
| + | + | + | + | + | + | - | + | + | - | + | | + | - | + | + | + | - | + | - | - | + | - |
| + | - | + | - | + | + | + | + | + | + | - | | + | - | - | + | - | + | - | + | + | + | + |
| + | - | + | - | - | + | - | + | - | - | - | | + | - | - | + | - | + | - | - | - | + | - |
| + | + | - | + | + | + | + | - | + | + | + | | + | + | + | - | + | + | + | + | + | - | + |
| + | + | - | + | + | - | - | - | + | - | + | | + | - | + | - | + | - | + | - | + | - | - |
| + | + | - | - | + | + | + | - | + | + | - | | + | + | + | - | - | + | - | + | + | - | + |
| + | + | - | - | + | - | - | - | - | - | - | | + | + | + | - | - | + | - | - | + | - | - |

By means of the tabular method it is possible to show that the definiendum and the definiens of each definition in the axiomatic system of this book has exactly the same SQS constellation. For example:

Table V:

| A | p | q | ↔ | $\bar{K}$ | $\bar{p}$ | $\bar{q}$ | | E | p | q | ↔ | $\bar{A}$ | $\bar{A}$ | $\bar{p}$ | q | $\bar{A}$ | p | $\bar{q}$ |
|---|---|---|---|---|---|---|---|---|---|---|---|---|---|---|---|---|---|---|
| + | + | + | | + | - | - | | + | + | + | | + | - | - | + | - | + | - |
| + | + | - | | + | - | + | | - | + | - | | - | + | - | - | - | + | + |
| + | - | + | | + | + | - | | - | - | + | | - | - | + | + | + | - | - |
| - | - | - | | - | + | + | | + | - | - | | + | - | + | - | - | - | + |

The definiendum and the definiens in each above definition being characterized by exactly the same SQS constellation means that they represent interchangeable WFOFs. If they are linked with the bijunctor, the resulting complex compound formula proves to be a tautology.

The achievement of ultimate SQS constellations by the full tabular method can be expedited in the following way:

(1) Place the appropriate leading columns under the first elementary formula on the left-hand side of the formula to be tested.

(2) Write the signs which those contained in the column already warrant under the junctor governing this elementary formula.

(3) Write the signs which those under this junctor already warrant under the junctor governing the compound formed by it and continue the procedure as far as possible.

(4) Omit any entry on the right-hand side of the first leading column which is not required for the matrix on its left-hand side.

(5) If required, write the appropriate signs under the next elementary formula and repeat the procedure under (3) and (4) until the SQS constellation under the first junctor of the formula to be tested is complete.

The following table illustrates this technique:

Table VI:

| C | K | Ā | p | q | D | q | r | E | r | p |
|---|---|---|---|---|---|---|---|---|---|---|
| + | − | − | + | | | | | | | |
| + | − | − | + | | | | | | | |
| + | − | − | + | | | | | | | |
| + | − | − | + | | | | | | | |
| + | − | − | − | + | | | | | | |
| + | − | − | − | + | | | | | | |
| + | − | + | − | − | − | − | + | | | |
| − | + | + | − | − | + | − | − | − | + | − |

This mechanical procedure can be applied to any WFOF. Still shorter non-mechanical ways are sometimes (as also here) available.

To test by means of the tabular method whether the conclusion of an inference is either valid or invalid, either solid or insolid, the inference must be expressed in the *statement form*. In this form it appears as a formula whose first junctor is the subjunctor. The consequent of the corresponding subjunction represents the conclusion and the antecedent of it represents the derivation base of the inference. A way to indicate that a formula is meant to be the expression of an inference is the following: A stroke ( / ) is placed immediately after the first junctor ( C ) and " /.'. " is placed immediately before the formula representing the conclusion of the inference. For example:

C/KKCpqCrsApr/.'.Aqs

If the total formula representing the inference proves to be a tautology, the conclusion of this inference is valid; otherwise it is invalid. If the formula representing the derivation base of the inference proves to be a dyslogy, the conclusion of this inference is insolid; otherwise it is solid. The conclusion of an inference is both valid and solid if the total formula representing the inference is a tautology and the formula representing the derivation base is not a dyslogy. If the latter proves to be a tautology , the formula representing the conclusion of the corresponding inference, if it is valid, must be a tautology.

For predicational calculus there is no procedure which would give an advance guarantee for *any* conclusion of a predicational inference that it is either valid or invalid. Nevertheless the tabular method (or other methods) can be employed for a part of predicational calculus to decide whether a given WFEF represents either a valid or invalid, either solid or insolid conclusion. This is feasible where the universe to which an inference relates can be assumed as non-empty and where the quantified compound predications formed by the junctors can be converted into those which contain only stigmic hypotacts. The resulting formulae can then be treated as indicatives to which the truth-values can be assigned. The requisite procedure proves to be inconvenient. For this reason no illustration of the corresponding procedure is provided here. The counter-formula method to be presented in the next chapter provides a far more convenient decision-procedure for the relevant part of predicational calculus.

### *4. The Short-cut Tabular Method*

The full tabular method offers a convenient procedure only where a few elementary formulae are involved in the expression of an inference. It may prove to be extremely cumbrous and lengthy where more complex formulae are involved. Thus a formula containing seven elementary formulae (which is not unusual in juristic inferences) would require a table with 128 rows for determining whether or not it is a tautology or a dyslogy. There is another, for many purposes a far more efficient, method for determining the ultimate SQS constellation of a formula - the short-cut tabular method ( STM ). Unfortunately it is not expedient in every case for reasons given below. The technique of the STM rests on the principles extracted from Table II in the previous section and lies in the observance of the following instructions:

I. For ascertaining whether a formula is a tautology:

(1) Treat any literal with an even number of bars as one without a bar and any literal with an odd number of bars as one with a single bar.

(2) Ascribe minus to the first junctor of the formula to be tested.

(3) Ascribe either minus or plus to the formula governed by this junctor as is necessary for yielding minus under it.

(4) Proceed to ascribe either plus or minus to the further component formulae as is necessary for yielding the signs already ascribed.

(5) Where at any stage of the procedure a sign was necessarily ascribed to a small literal, ascribe the same sign to the same literal wherever occurring and ascribe the opposite sign to its negation.

(6) Ascribe the appropriate signs to the junctors wherever this is possible.

(7) Proceed with Instructions (3), (4), or (5) in any order until no further step is compelled by them.

The procedure yields the following possibilities:

(a) If the signs were ascribed consistently and minus under the first junctor can stand, the formula tested is either a dyslogy or an amphilogy.

(b) If the procedure leads to some inconsistency (viz. the sign ascribed to a junctor proves to be incorrect, the sign required for a small literal is opposite to the one previously ascribed to the same literal, or a formula and its negation require the ascription of the same sign), the formula tested is a tautology.

(c) If the procedure leads to a situation in which there is no compulsion to ascribe the signs, this procedure is inapplicable. In this case it becomes necessary either to resort to another decision-procedure (e.g. to the full tabular method) or to test by the above method all possible ascriptions until their possibilities are exhausted. If none of them yields minus under the first junctor of the formula tested, this formula is a tautology; otherwise it is either a dyslogy or an amphilogy.

II. For ascertaining whether a formula is a dyslogy:

Follow the same procedure with the dyslogy test proviso (D.T.P.).

D.T.P.: Ascribe plus to the first junctor of the formula to be tested.

The procedure leads to the following possibilities:

(a) If the signs were ascribed consistently and plus under the first junctor can stand, the formula tested is either a tautology or an amphilogy.

(b) If the procedure leads to some inconsistency, the formula tested is a dyslogy.

(c) If the procedure leads to a situation in which there is no compulsion to ascribe the signs, this procedure is inapplicable. If by the above method all possible ascriptions are tested until their possibilities are exhausted then if none of them yields plus under the first junctor of the formula tested, this formula is a dyslogy; otherwise it is either a tautology or an amphilogy.

III. For ascertaining whether a formula is an amphilogy:

Perform both the tautology test and the dyslogy test.

The procedure leads to the following possibilities:

(a) The formula tested is proved to be a tautology.

(b) The formula tested is proved to be a dyslogy.

(c) The formula tested is proved to be neither a tautology nor a dyslogy, in which case it is an amphilogy.

The following examples illustrate the STM:

Test whether $C \bar{\bar{K}} C p \bar{\bar{\bar{q}}} C \bar{q} r C p \bar{\bar{r}}$ is a tautology!

```
1 : C K C p q̄ C q̄ r C p r
```
(1).

```
2 : C K C p q̄ C q̄ r C p r
    -
```
(2).

```
3 : C K C p q̄ C q̄ r C p r
    - +           -
```
(3). C can have minus only if the first formula it governs has plus and the second has minus.

```
4 : C K C p q̄ C q̄ r C p r
    - + +     +     -
```
(4). K can have plus only if both formulae it governs have plus.

```
5 : C K C p q̄ C q̄ r C p r
    - + +     +     - + -
```
(4) applied to C p r .

```
6 : C K C p q̄ C q̄ r C p r
    - + + +   +   - - + -
```
(5). By Step 5, plus and minus were ascribed to p and r respectively; therefore the same signs must be ascribed to the same literals throughout the formula.

7 : $CKCp\bar{q}C\bar{q}rCpr$ — (4) applied to $Cp\bar{q}$ , where both the subjunctor and the antecedent of the subjunction already have plus.

| C | K | C | p | $\bar{q}$ | C | $\bar{q}$ | r | C | p | r |
|---|---|---|---|---|---|---|---|---|---|---|
| − | + | + | + | + | + |  | − | − | + | − |

8 : $CKCp\bar{q}C\bar{q}rCpr$ — (5) applied to $C\bar{q}r$ , because plus was ascribed to q by Step 7.

| C | K | C | p | $\bar{q}$ | C | $\bar{q}$ | r | C | p | r |
|---|---|---|---|---|---|---|---|---|---|---|
| − | + | + | + | + | + | + | − | − | + | − |
| 2 | 3 | 4 | 6 | 7 | 4 | 8 | 6 | 3 | 5 | 5 |

The numbers indicate the steps by which each sign was ascribed.

The last step produces an inconsistency in the ascription of the signs. The place at which the inconsistency occurs is indicated by a half-frame. This result brings out that the initial ascription of minus to the first junctor of the tested formula was impossible. Consequently, only pluses can occur under this junctor and the formula is a tautology.

Test whether $KKKDpqCrs\bar{A}\bar{q}\bar{s}r$ is a dyslogy!

| K | K | K | D | p | q | C | r | s | $\bar{A}$ | $\bar{q}$ | $\bar{s}$ | r |
|---|---|---|---|---|---|---|---|---|---|---|---|---|
| + | + | + | + | + | + | + | + | + | + | − | − | + |
| 1 | 2 | 3 | 4 | 7 | 6 | 4 | 9 | 8 | 3 | 5 | 5 | 2 |

This test produced no inconsistency. Thus plus under the first junctor of the formula can occur. Therefore, the tested formula is not a dyslogy; it is either a tautology or an amphilogy.

Test whether $CKE\bar{p}\bar{q}KCqr\bar{A}AsvwApq$ is an amphilogy!

Tautology Test:

| C | K | E | $\bar{p}$ | $\bar{q}$ | K | C | q | r | $\bar{A}$ | A | s | v | w | A | p | q |
|---|---|---|---|---|---|---|---|---|---|---|---|---|---|---|---|---|
| − | + | + | + | + | + | + | − | − | + | − | − | − | − | − | − | − |
| 1 | 2 | 3 | 8 | 8 | 3 | 4 | 9 | 10 | 4 | 5 | 7 | 7 | 5 | 2 | 6 | 6 |

This test produced no inconsistency. Therefore, the tested formula is not a tautology.

Dyslogy Test:

| C | K | E | $\bar{p}$ | $\bar{q}$ | K | C | q | r | $\bar{A}$ | A | s | v | w | A | p | q |
|---|---|---|---|---|---|---|---|---|---|---|---|---|---|---|---|---|
| + | − | + | + | + | − | + | − | − | − | − | − | − | + | − | − | − |
| 1 | 2 | 5 | 4 | 4 | 6 | 8 | 7 | 9 | 10 | 12 | 13 | 14 | 11 | 2 | 3 | 3 |

This test, too, produced no inconsistency. Therefore, the tested formula is not a dyslogy either. Consequently, it must be an amphilogy. Note that a number of ascriptions here were not compulsory (viz. those by Steps 2, 9, 11, and 12), but they were all possible ascriptions.

There are cases in which the STM succeeds in identifying a formula as either tautologous or dyslogous even though the signs are not ascribed to every part of it.

Further there are cases in which this identification is not possible with a single line. The following example provides an illustration for both cases.

Test whether $A\bar{E}pApKpq\bar{C}pApr$ is a dyslogy!

| A | Ē | p | A | p | K | p | q | C̄ | p | A | p | r |
|---|---|---|---|---|---|---|---|---|---|---|---|---|
| +1 | +2 | | | | | | | +2 | [+3] | −3 | [−4] | |
| +1 | +2 | [+3] | −3 | [−4] | −4 | | | −2 | | | | |
| +1 | +2 | [−3] | +3 | −4 | +5 | [+6] | | −2 | | | | |
| +1 | −2 | | | | | | | +2 | [+3] | −3 | [−4] | |

Since the first junctor of the tested formula is an adjunctor, the ascription of plus to it opens three ascription possibilities by Step 2. All these had to be examined. They all lead to inconsistencies. Therefore, the tested formula is a dyslogy.

There are formulae which require a considerable number of lines for the application of the STM, in which case this method is of little practical value. The following formula provides an example for such a case if it is to be subjected to a dyslogy test:

$$\bar{K}ACpqACq\bar{r}KA\bar{s}vwKrs$$

To determine whether a conclusion of an inference is either valid or invalid, solid or insolid by the STM, the inference is to be expressed in its statement form. If the corresponding formula proves to be a tautology, the conclusion is valid; otherwise it is invalid. If the part of the formula which represents the derivation base of the inference proves to be a dyslogy, the conclusion is insolid; otherwise it is solid.

Since the STM is based on the full tabular method, the same transformation of formulae as described in the previous section is required for making it applicable as a decision-procedure for a part of predicational calculus. Here, too, the requisite procedure proves to be rather inconvenient and thus the counter-formula method is to be preferred to the STM for effecting logical decisions.

## IV. THE COUNTER-FORMULA METHOD AS A DECISION-PROCEDURE

### 1. *The Basic Framework of the Counter-formula Method*

The counter-formula method ( CFM ) is a procedure by means of which it is possible to decide above all whether a formula is either a tautology or a dyslogy or an amphilogy and whether the claimed conclusion of an inference is either valid or invalid, either solid or insolid. The CFM leads fast to the breaking of long formulae into short ones and its procedure is easily surveyable. Clerical errors that may have occurred in the columns of its deduction are relatively easy to detect. Its rules are simple and few in number. Their application is not difficult. Thus the CFM proves to be an efficient as well as expedient decision-procedure both for theoretical and practical purposes in the field of law.

In the following exposition of the basic framework of the CFM, the letters $X$ , $Y$ , and $Z$ are employed to stand for *any* well-formed formula (be it elementary or compound). Thus $X$ stands for $p$ , but also for $Cpq$ , $KpEpq$ , etc. In the context of the CFM, "counter-formula" ( CF ) means a formula which differs from another formula by one bar on top of its first component. Thus $\bar{X}$ is a CF of $X$ and vice versa and $\bar{K}X\bar{Y}$ is a CF of $\bar{\bar{K}}X\bar{Y}$ and vice versa. A formula and its counter-formula stand in a formula counter-formula relationship, which is signified here by the abbreviation "F-CF".

The instrumentarium of the CFM contains transcription rules ( T.R.s ), elimination rules ( E.R.s ), and the rule of position rearrangement ( R.P.R. ). By the T.R.s, all junctions other than adjunctions or conjunctions can be expressed either as adjunctions or as conjunctions. By the elimination rules ( E.R.s ), shorter formulae are achieved either directly or indirectly. By the R.P.R. the components of a formula can be so organized that, if required, application of further rules of the CFM becomes possible. The goal of the CFM is achieved either when the application of the relevant rules brings forth a counter-formula to any formula appearing in the derivation procedure or when after the exhaustion of all applicable rules this proves to be unfeasible.

*Transcription Rules:*

(1) Replace $C X Y$ with $A \bar{X} Y$ (Subjunction Duality - S.Dual.)

(2) Replace $D X Y$ with $A X \bar{Y}$ (Dejunction Duality - D.Dual.)

(3) Replace $E X Y$ with $K A \bar{X} Y A X \bar{Y}$ (Bijunction Dissection - B.Diss.)

(4) Replace $\bar{C} X Y$ with $K X \bar{Y}$ (Contrasubjunction Duality - CS.Dual.)

(5) Replace $\bar{D} X Y$ with $K \bar{X} Y$ (Contradejunction Duality - CD.Dual.)

(6) Replace $\bar{A} X Y$ with $K \bar{X} \bar{Y}$ (Contraadjunction Duality - CA.Dual.)

(7) Replace $\bar{K} X Y$ with $A \bar{X} \bar{Y}$ (Contraconjunction Duality - CC.Dual.)

(8) Replace $\bar{E} X Y$ with $K A X Y A \bar{X} \bar{Y}$ (Contrabijunction Dissection - CB.Diss.)

*Elimination Rules:*

(1) Wherever more bars than one occur on top of a literal, write the literal with no bar in case of an even number of bars and with one bar in case of an odd number of bars. (Double Negation - D.N.)

For example, from $\bar{\bar{X}}$ follows $X$ ; from $\bar{\bar{\bar{X}}}$ follows $\bar{X}$

(2) Wherever in an adjunction the same adjunct occurs twice, cancel the adjunctor and one adjunct and write the remaining formula. (Autology - Aut.)

For example, from $A X X$ follows $X$

(3) Wherever a conjunction occurs as a separate entry, write any conjunct separately. (Conjunction Elimination - C.E.)

For example, from $K X K Y Z$ follows $X$ , $Y$ , or $Z$

(4) Wherever an adjunction containing a conjunction occurs as a separate entry, cancel the conjunctor and one conjunct and write the remaining formula. (Conjunction Contraction - C.C.)

For example, from $A X K Y Z$ follows $A X Y$ or $A X Z$

(5) Wherever an adjunction and the counter-formula of one of its adjuncts occur as separate entries, write the other adjunct. (Adjunction Elimination - A.E.)

For example, from $A X Y$ and $\bar{X}$ follows $Y$

(6) Wherever two adjunctions occur as separate entries and one adjunct in one adjunction has a counter-formula in the other adjunction, write an adjunction which contains the remaining adjuncts. (Adjunction Contraction - A.C.)

For example, from $AXY$ and $A\bar{X}Z$ follows $AYZ$

*Rule of Position Rearrangement:*

In every adjunction or in every conjunction, the position of its adjunctors or adjuncts and of its conjunctors or conjuncts can be freely rearranged under the rules which determine the well-formed formulae. (R.P.R.)

For example, from $AXAXY$ follows $AAXXY$ or $AYAXX$

The procedure of the CFM can be expedited by applying the following auxiliary elimination rules:

(1) Wherever an adjunction contains a conjunction whose one conjunct is a counter-formula of the other conjunct, cancel the adjunctor and the conjunction and write the remaining adjunct. (Dyslogy Elimination - D.E.)

For example, from $AXKY\bar{Y}$ follows $X$

(2) Wherever an adjunction occurs as a separate entry and contains a conjunction for one of whose conjuncts a counter-formula occurs as a separate entry, write the other adjunct. (Conjunctive Adjunction Elimination - C.A.E.)

For example, from $AXKYZ$ and $\bar{Z}$ follows $X$

(3) Wherever two adjunctions having a common adjunct occur as separate entries whose other adjuncts are a formula and a counter-formula to each other, write the common adjunct. (Autological Adjunction Contraction - A.A.C.)

For example, from $AXY$ and $A\bar{X}Y$ follows $Y$

In the course of the procedure of the CFM certain derivations may occur which contribute in no way to the achievement of the goal of the method. The corresponding entries can be omitted by virtue of the following sparing rules ( S.R.s ):

(1) Omit those entries which are recognizable as tautologies.

(2) Omit those entries which have already occurred in the procedure.

(3) Omit those adjunctive entries whose one adjunct has already occurred as an entry in the procedure.

In applying S.R.(1), note that a formula is tautologous if it is an adjunction whose one adjunct is a counter-formula of the other adjunct.

## 2. *The Counter-formula Method Applied in Propositional Calculus*

The procedure of the counter-formula method has the following pattern: In the derivation column, first the formula to be tested, or the derivation base of the argument to be examined, is written; after the corresponding entry or entries the formulae are written which result from the application of the relevant CFM rules. The justification column contains the information about the entries in the derivation column. In order to avoid long formulae or trivial entries as much as possible, several steps can be combined. Thus when the rules of dissection are applied, they can always be combined with the application of C.E. Also the application of D.N. can always be combined with any step. If the application of C.E. yields several short formulae, it is advisable (to save the space) to write the conjuncts on the same line one after the other separated by commas. If the same rule finds a repeated application in the same step, it needs to be indicated only once.

Tautology Test:

The first entry in the derivation column is here the formula to be tested. The next entry is its counter-formula indicated by "CF" in the justification column. Thereafter the requisite rules of the CFM are applied to the latter and to the subsequent formulae. If in the procedure a CF appears for any entry after the second one, the tested formula is a tautology. If after the exhaustion of all applicable rules this does not occur, it is either a dyslogy or an amphilogy.

Determine whether $A\overline{K}CpqA\overline{q}r\overline{K}p\overline{r}$ is a tautology!

| | | |
|---|---|---|
| 1. | $A\overline{K}CpqA\overline{q}r\overline{K}p\overline{r}$ | |
| 2. | $\overline{A}\overline{K}CpqA\overline{q}r\overline{K}p\overline{r}$ | 1, CF |
| 3. | $KKCpqA\overline{q}rKp\overline{r}$ | 2, CA.Dual., D.N. |
| 4. | $A\overline{p}q$ | 3, C.E., S.Dual. |

5. $A \bar{q} r$      3, C.E.

6. $p, \bar{r}$      3, C.E.

7. $q$      4,6, A.E.

8. $\bar{q}$      5,6, A.E.

7,8: F-CF

Therefore, the tested formula is a tautology.

Dyslogy Test:

The first entry in the derivation column is also here the formula to be tested. To this formula the relevant rules of the CFM are directly applied. If in the procedure a CF appears for any subsequent entry, the tested formula is a dyslogy. If after the exhaustion of all applicable rules this does not occur, it is either a tautology or an amphilogy.

Determine whether $\bar{C} K C p q C q r C p r$ is a dyslogy!

1. $\bar{C} K C p q C q r C p r$

2. $K K C p q C q r \bar{C} p r$      1, CS.Dual.

3. $A \bar{p} q$      2, C.E., S.Dual.

4. $A \bar{q} r$      2, C.E., S.Dual.

5. $K p \bar{r}$      2, C.E., S.Dual.

6. $p, \bar{r}$      5, C.E.

7. $q$      3,6, A.E.

8. $\bar{q}$      4,6, A.E.

7,8: F-CF

Therefore, the tested formula is a dyslogy.

Amphilogy Test:

That a formula is an amphilogy is proved by subjecting it to both the tautology test and the dyslogy test and by ascertaining that it is neither a tautology nor a dyslogy.

Determine whether $C K D \bar{p} q D q r C p r$ is an amphilogy!

A Negative Tautology Proof

1. $C K D \bar{p} q D q r C p r$

2. $\bar{C}KD\bar{p}qDqrCpr$ CF

3. $KKA\bar{p}\bar{q}Aq\bar{r}Kp\bar{r}$ 2, CS.Dual., D.Dual.

4. $A\bar{p}\bar{q}$ 3, C.E.

5. $Aq\bar{r}$ 3, C.E.

6. $A\bar{p}\bar{r}$ 4,5, A.C.

7. $p, \bar{r}$ 3, C.E.

8. $\bar{q}$ 4,7, A.E.

F-CF unattainable

Therefore, the tested formula is not a tautology.

A Negative Dyslogy Proof:

1. $CKD\bar{p}qDqrCpr$

2. $A\bar{K}D\bar{p}qDqrA\bar{p}r$ 1, S.Dual.

3. $AA\bar{D}\bar{p}q\bar{D}qrA\bar{p}r$ 2, CC.Dual.

4. $AAKpqK\bar{q}rA\bar{p}r$ 3, CD.Dual., D.N.

5. $AAA\bar{p}rqr$ 4, C.C., R.P.R.

6. $AA\bar{p}qr$ 5, Aut.

F-CF unattainable

Therefore, the tested formula is not a dyslogy.

Because both proofs led to a negative result, and thus the tested formula is neither a tautology nor a dyslogy, this formula must be an amphilogy.

In order to ascertain whether the conclusion of an inference is either valid or invalid or whether it is either solid or insolid, a derivation schema is used which is similar to that employed in the ordinary deductive proofs.

Where either the validity or the invalidity of a conclusion is to be determined, the first entry after the last premiss of the inference is the counter-formula of the conclusion ( CFC ). If the procedure leads to a CF for any entry in the derivation column, the conclusion is valid. If after the exhaustion of all applicable rules of the CFM this result cannot be achieved, the conclusion is invalid.

A Validity Proof:

1. $C p q$
2. $\bar{K} q \bar{r}$ $\quad$ /∴ $\underline{C p r}$
3. $\bar{C} p r$ $\quad$ CFC
4. $K p \bar{r}$ $\quad$ 3, CS.Dual.
5. $p , \bar{r}$ $\quad$ 4, C.E.
6. $A \bar{p} q$ $\quad$ 1, S.Dual.
7. $A \bar{q} r$ $\quad$ 2, CC.Dual., D.N.
8. $q$ $\quad$ 6,5, A.E.
9. $\bar{q}$ $\quad$ 7,5, A.E.

8,9: F-CF

Therefore, the conclusion of this inference is valid.

An Invalidity Proof:

1. $\bar{K} p \bar{q}$
2. $D \bar{r} \bar{q}$ $\quad$ /∴ $\underline{C p r}$
3. $\bar{C} p r$ $\quad$ CFC
4. $K p \bar{r}$ $\quad$ 3, CS.Dual.
5. $p , \bar{r}$ $\quad$ 4, C.E.
6. $A \bar{p} q$ $\quad$ 1, CC.Dual., D.N.
7. $q$ $\quad$ 6,5, A.E.

F-CF unattainable

Therefore, the conclusion of this inference is invalid.

Where either the solidity or the insolidity of a conclusion is to be determined, the rules of the CFM are directly applied to the premiss or premisses of the inference (i.e. CFC is not inserted in the derivation column here). If the procedure leads to a CF of any formula in the derivation column, the conclusion is insolid. If after the exhaustion of all applicable rules this result cannot be achieved, the conclusion is solid.

An Insolidity Proof:

1. C p q
2. $\bar{A}$ r q
3. p    /.'. K q $\bar{r}$

4. A $\bar{p}$ q    1, S.Dual.
5. q    4,3, A.E.
6. K $\bar{r}$ $\bar{q}$    2, CA.Dual.
7. $\bar{q}$    6, C.E.

5,7: F-CF

Therefore, the conclusion of this inference is insolid.

A Solidity Proof:

1. D p $\bar{q}$
2. C p r
3. $\bar{K}$ $\bar{q}$ $\bar{s}$    /.'. A q r

4. A p q    1, D.Dual., D.N.
5. A $\bar{p}$ r    2, S.Dual.
6. A q r    4,5, A.C.
7. A q s    3, CC.Dual., D.N.

F-CF unattainable

Therefore, the conclusion of this inference is solid.

### 3. *The Counter-formula Method Applied in Predicational Calculus*

As a decision-procedure, the counter-formula method finds a limited application also in predicational calculus. Although there is no method making a logical decision possible for *every* predicational conclusion, logical decisions can be achieved here, too, in certain areas. In any event, the application of the CFM in predicational calculus makes it possible to ascertain, whether the negation of the conclusion of an inference is either consistent or inconsistent with its derivation base. If it proves to be inconsistent, the argument examined cannot be regarded as sound. This result is of considerable practical significance for legal reasoning.

Apart from the instrumentarium of propositional calculus supplied in the previous section, recourse to the following principles is needed in the application of the CFM in predicational calculus:

(1) The rules of Universal Stigmication and of Particular Stigmication.

(2) The theorems of Universalizer Negation and of Particularizer Negation.

(3) Those theorems of Quantor Location which relate to predicational adjunctions, viz. $C\,A\,{\wedge}F\,{\wedge}G\,{\wedge}A\,F\,G$ and $C\,A\,{\vee}F\,{\vee}G\,{\vee}A\,F\,G$ (a derivate of $E\,A\,{\vee}F\,{\vee}G\,{\vee}A\,F\,G$).

The corresponding theorems relating to predicational conjunctions are dispensable, because the conjuncts can be written separately under the rule of C.E. and can then be stigmicated.

(4) The relatorial properties as a basis of relational inferences.

In addition to the above four principles, recourse to the concept of extended counter-formula makes some applications of the CFM expedient in predicational calculus. The corresponding principle ( ECF ) can be formulated as follows:

> A universalized formula and its corresponding singular formula are a F-CF to each other if their predicators or their first junctors differ from each other only by a bar. (ECF)

For example, $\wedge_{x}\bar{F}x$ and $Fa$ ; $\wedge_{x}C\,Fx\,\bar{G}x$ and $\bar{C}\,Fx\,\bar{G}x$

A Validity Proof:

| | | |
|---|---|---|
| 1. | $\bar{\vee}_{x}\vee_{y}K\,Fx\,\bar{G}y$ | |
| 2. | $\bar{C}\,Fa\,\bar{H}e$ | $/\therefore$ $Ge$ |
| 3. | $\bar{G}e$ | CFC |
| 4. | $\wedge_{x}\wedge_{y}\bar{K}\,Fx\,\bar{G}y$ | 1, P.N. |
| 5. | $\bar{K}\,Fa\,\bar{G}e$ | 4, U.T. |

| | | |
|---|---|---|
| 6. | $A\ \bar{F}a\ Ge$ | 5, CC Dual., D.N. |
| 7. | $\bar{F}a$ | 6,3, A.E. |
| 8. | $K\ Fa\ He$ | 2, CS.Dual., D.N. |
| 9. | $Fa$ | 8, C.E. |

7,9: F-CF

Therefore, the conclusion of this inference is valid.

An Invalidity Proof:

| | | |
|---|---|---|
| 1. | $A\ \bar{F}a\ \underset{xy}{\wedge\wedge}\bar{D}\ \bar{F}x\ Sxy$ | |
| 2. | $C\ \underset{xz}{\vee\vee}\bar{R}xz\ \underset{x}{\wedge}Fx$ | |
| 3. | $D\ \bar{F}a\ Sae$ | |
| ( 4. | R - Sym. ) | /∴ $Sea$ |
| 5. | $\bar{S}ea$ | CFC |
| 6. | $\bar{F}a$ | 1,3, ECF, A.E. |
| 7. | $A\ \underset{xz}{\bar{\vee}\vee}\bar{R}xz\ \underset{x}{\wedge}Fx$ | 2, S.Dual. |
| 8. | $A\ \underset{xz}{\wedge\wedge}Rxz\ \underset{x}{\vee}Fx$ | 7, P.N., D.N. |
| 9. | $\underset{xz}{\wedge\wedge}A\ Rxz\ Fx$ | 8, Q.L. |
| 10. | $A\ Rao\ Fa$ | 9, P.T. |
| 11. | $Rao$ | 6,10, A.E. |
| 12. | $Rou$ | 11, Sym. |
| 13. | $K\ \bar{F}a\ \bar{S}ae$ | 3, D.Dual. |
| 14. | $\bar{S}ae$ | 13, C.E. |

F-CF unattainable

Therefore, the conclusion of this inference is invalid.

A Solidity Proof:

| | | |
|---|---|---|
| 1. | $D\ \wedge F\ \vee G$ | |
| 2. | $\bar{\wedge}C\ \bar{H}\ F$ | |
| 3. | $\bar{C}\ \bar{G}a\ Ha$ | /∴ $Ga$ |
| 4. | $A\ \wedge F\ \bar{\vee}G$ | 1, D.Dual. |
| 5. | $A\ \wedge F\ \wedge\bar{G}$ | 4, P.N. |

| | | |
|---|---|---|
| 6. | $\wedge A\ F\ \bar{G}$ | 5, Q.L. |
| 7. | $\vee \bar{C}\ \bar{H}\ F$ | 2, U.N. |
| 8. | $\bar{C}\ \bar{H}e\ Fe$ | 7, P.T. |
| 9. | $K\ \bar{H}e\ \bar{F}e$ | 8, CS.Dual. |
| 10. | $\bar{H}e\ ,\ \bar{F}e$ | 9, C.E. |
| 11. | $A\ Fe\ \bar{G}e$ | 6, U.T. |
| 12. | $\bar{G}e$ | 11,10, A.E. |
| 13. | $K\ \bar{G}a\ \bar{H}a$ | 3, CS.Dual. |
| 14. | $\bar{G}a\ ,\ \bar{H}a$ | 13, C.E. |

F-CF unattainable

Therefore, the conclusion of this inference is solid.

An Insolidity Proof:

| | | |
|---|---|---|
| 1. | $\bigwedge\bigwedge\bigwedge_{xyz} \bar{A}\ \bar{R}xy\ \bar{R}yz$ | |
| 2. | $D\ Rei\ Rai$ | |
| 3. | $\bar{R}ie$ | |
| ( 4. | R - Sym.,Trans. ) /.'. | $Roe$ |
| 5. | $\bar{A}\ \bar{R}ae\ \bar{R}ei$ | 1, U.T. |
| 6. | $K\ Rae\ Rei$ | 5, CA.Dual., D.N. |
| 7. | $Rai$ | 6, Trans. |
| 8. | $A\ Rei\ \bar{R}ai$ | 2, D.Dual. |
| 9. | $Rei$ | 8,7, A.E. |
| 10. | $Rie$ | 9, Sym. |

7,10: F-CF

Therefore, the conclusion of this inference is insolid.

## 4. *Strategy and Further Applications of the Counter-formula Method*

It is possible, of course, to exhaust first the application of the transcription rules and then to apply the elimination rules. This course of action is, however, not always the simplest and the shortest way to reach the goal of the counter-formula method. Accordingly, it is advisable to apply the relevant E.R.s as soon as this can be done. In this way shorter and better surveyable formulae are produced. The most expedient procedure consists in a purposeful combination of the application of both groups of rules. The requisite skill can be acquired through practice.

The premisses of an inference can be treated in any sequence by the CFM. However, for the purposes of the tests or proofs such as those presented in the two previous sections, it is advisable to start with shorter formulae and then to proceed to longer formulae, unless the latter are conjunctions amenable to the application of C.E. Proceeding in this manner, some otherwise requisite steps may prove unnecessary under S.R.s and shorter formulae may be achieved at the earliest possible stage. As long as the goal of the method has not been achieved, no premiss can be excluded from the treatment. By striving for elementary or simple formulae as soon as possible, the most efficient use is made of S.R.(3).

The validity-invalidity and solidity-insolidity proofs can be performed in a *consolidated procedure*. This procedure starts with the latter kind of proof. If the claimed conclusion proves to be solid, a line is drawn under the last entry of the derivation column and immediately below the line the counter-formula of the claimed conclusion is written. The consolidated procedure avoids a repetitious writing of entries, which would be required if the two kinds of proof are conducted separately. In propositional calculus, the consolidated procedure can be carried out in a straightforward manner. In predicational calculus, it is important to pay special attention to the observance of predicational rules of derivation in the phase of validity-invalidity proof. This may require that certain steps in this phase are numbered as consecutive to the number of the last premiss of the examined inference. Thus if the inference has two premisses, the first entry under the line is numbered as " 2a ".

Examples of the Consolidated Procedure:

| | | |
|---|---|---|
| 1. | $D K p q r$ | |
| 2. | $K s \bar{v}$ | |
| 3. | $C s K p \bar{r}$ | |
| 4. | $C \bar{r} K p w$ | /∴ $A s K p \bar{r}$ |
| 5. | $A K p q \bar{r}$ | 1, D.Dual. |
| 6. | $s , \bar{v}$ | 2, C.E. |
| 7. | $A s K p \bar{r}$ | 3, S.Dual. |
| 8. | $A r K p w$ | 4, S.Dual., D.N. |
| 9. | $p , \bar{r}$ | 7,6, A.E., C.E. |
| 10. | $w$ | 8,9, A.E., C.E. |

Solid: F-CF unattainable

| | | |
|---|---|---|
| 11. | $\bar{A} s K p \bar{r}$ | CFC |

Valid: 7,11: F-CF

| | | |
|---|---|---|
| 1. | $\wedge C\ F\ G$ | |
| 2. | $\vee \bar{K}\ G\ H$ | /∴ $\wedge A\ \bar{F}\ \bar{H}$ |
| 3. | $\bar{K}\ Ga\ Ha$ | 2, P.T. |
| 4. | $A\ \bar{G}a\ \bar{H}a$ | 3, CC.Dual. |
| 5. | $C\ Fa\ Ga$ | 1, U.T. |
| 6. | $A\ \bar{F}a\ Ga$ | 5, S.Dual. |
| 7. | $A\ \bar{F}a\ \bar{H}a$ | 6,4, A.C. |

Solid: F-CF unattainable

| | | |
|---|---|---|
| 2a. | $\bar{\wedge} A\ \bar{F}\ \bar{H}$ | CFC |
| 2b. | $\vee \bar{A}\ \bar{F}\ \bar{H}$ | 2a, U.N. |
| 2c. | $\bar{A}\ \bar{F}e\ \bar{H}e$ | 2b, P.T. |
| 2d. | $Fe\ ,\ He$ | 2c, CA.Dual., D.N., C.E. |

Invalid: F-CF unattainable

Apart from the applications of the CFM considered so far, the method can render further services, which are valuable also for the lawyer. These include answers to the following questions:

(1) Is the conclusion of an inference self-contradictory?

(2) Is any premiss of an inference self-contradictory?

(3) Is the conclusion of an inference analytic truth?

(4) Is any premiss of an inference analytic truth?

(5) Is the conclusion of an inference compatible with its derivation base?

(6) Is any premiss of an inference redundant?

In order to answer (1) and (2), the conclusion or premiss in question has to be subjected to a dyslogy test; in order to answer (3) and (4), the conclusion or premiss in question has to be subjected to a tautology test. It is obvious that a self-contradictory (i.e. dyslogous) statement is worthless for any proper legal purpose. An analytic (i.e. tautologous) statement represents only a trivial truth; a conclusion of that kind requires no proof under the theorem *Ex Quolibet Verum* .

In order to answer (5), the conclusion in question is to be subjected to a compatibility-incompatibility proof. This requires the insertion of the formula standing for the conclusion of the examined inference in the derivation column as the next entry after the last premiss of the inference; in the justification column it is indicated by the abbreviation "I.C." ("Inserted Conclusion"). If the proof produces a F-CF, the conclusion is incompatible with its derivation base. If after the exhaustion of all applicable rules of the CFM this result cannot be achieved, the conclusion is compatible with its derivation base.

In order to answer (6), it has to be ascertained in a validity proof whether the premiss in question has been used in the procedure. If it has not been used, in which case the number of the premiss does not appear in the justification column, the premiss is redundant. It may happen that either one or another premiss of an inference is redundant. It may also happen that a premiss is redundant where one set of premisses is used and another premiss is redundant where another set of premisses is used. In legal arguments redundant premisses occur quite frequently in order to provide alternative grounds for a judicial or other decision. This lack of *elegantia iuris* is harmless as long as redundant premisses do not produce the insolidity of conclusions. If this is their effect, especially if a redundant premiss proves to be also self-contradictory, redundancies have to be removed by appropriate legal techniques.

Examples for Discovery of Redundancies:

| | | |
|---|---|---|
| 1. | $CApqK\bar{r}s$ | |
| 2. | $CA\bar{q}\bar{v}w$ | |
| 3. | $Cp\bar{r}$ | /.'. $\underline{Crw}$ |
| 4. | $\bar{C}rw$ | CFC |
| 5. | $r , \bar{w}$ | 4, CS.Dual., C.E. |
| 6. | $AKqvw$ | 2, S.Dual., CA.Dual., D.N. |
| 7. | $Kqv$ | 6,5, A.E. |
| 8. | $q , v$ | 7, C.E. |
| 9. | $AK\bar{p}\bar{q}K\bar{r}s$ | 1, S.Dual., CA.Dual. |
| 10. | $A\bar{q}\bar{r}$ | 9, C.C. |
| 11. | $\bar{r}$ | 10,8, A.E. |

Valid: 5,11: F-CF

Because Premiss 3 does not appear in the justification column, it is redundant.

| | | |
|---|---|---|
| 1. | $Cpq$ | |
| 2. | $p$ | |
| 3. | $CKpqr$ | |
| 4. | $CK\bar{p}\bar{r}\bar{s}$ | /.'. $\underline{Csr}$ |

| | | | |
|---|---|---|---|
| Proof I: | 5. | $\bar{C}\ s\ r$ | CFC |
| | 6. | $s\ ,\ \bar{r}$ | 5, CS.Dual., C.E. |
| | 7. | $A\ \bar{p}\ q$ | 1, S.Dual. |
| | 8. | $A\ A\ \bar{p}\ \bar{q}\ r$ | 3, S.Dual., CC.Dual. |
| | 9. | $\bar{q}$ | 8,2,6, A.E. |
| | 10. | $\bar{p}$ | 7,9, A.E. |
| | Valid: | 2,10: F-CF | |
| Proof II: | 9. | $A\ \bar{K}\ \bar{p}\ \bar{r}\ \bar{s}$ | 4, S.Dual. |
| | 10. | $A\ A\ p\ r\ \bar{s}$ | 9, CC.Dual., D.N. |
| | 11. | $p$ | 10,6, A.E. |
| | 12. | $\bar{q}$ | 8,6,11, A.E. |
| | 13. | $\bar{p}$ | 7,12, A.E. |
| | Valid: | 11,13: F-CF | |

In Proof I, Premiss 4 proved to be redundant; in Proof II, Premiss 2 proved to be redundant.

# Part II

## Legal Logic in Action

## I. Logical Organization of Legal Language

### 1. *Problems with Operators*

This chapter is concerned with problems of the "translation" of legal language into symbolic expressions for logical purposes. The scope of legal language includes not only the language of legislative acts, of judgments, and of legal documents (i.e. the raw material of law) but also the language used in talking and writing about law. One of the most difficult tasks facing the application of logic in the field of law is the correct symbolic expression of legal language. This is partly due to general problems inherent in symbolizing ordinary language for logical purposes and partly due to the specific nature of legal language.

The symbols employed by logicians are artificial creations and thus capable of being endowed with desired precise meanings. Within the range of their application, they are not affected by the ambiguities, vaguenesses, and emotive overtones which abound in ordinary language. However, in putting ordinary language into symbols, the achievement of precision may often entail a loss in style: by using an artificial language free from the imperfections of ordinary language, the beauty which the original text may have cannot usually be preserved. This beauty, however, is not a concern of the logician.

Although the logical operators have precise meanings in the relevant system of logic, certain problems do arise in regard to the use of the correct operator in many cases. In the following, each operator is examined in turn. In legal usage, as in ordinary usage, propositions may be joined by words signifying logical operators and the combination may be stated in an abbreviated, elliptical form. For example, "This deed requires stamping and registration" is a convenient short way of saying "This deed requires stamping and this deed requires registration". Unless it is required for special reasons, the laborious expanded expression should be avoided and convenient elliptical expressions should be used. To achieve brevity, appropriate pronouns can also be employed instead of nouns or phrases.

The negation of a proposition is often expressed by inserting a "not" in the proposition; it is symbolized by placing a bar on top of the formula representing the negated proposition. If this proposition is elementary, the negator occurs on top of a small literal; if it is compound, the negator occurs on top of the first operator of the corresponding formula. Propositions which commence with phrases such as "It is not the case that ..." or "It is not true that ..." are obviously symbolized by the use of the negator on the first literal of the formula representing the negated proposition. Negation may further be expressed by using words such as "never", "nobody", and "nothing". It is clear that by symbolizing a proposition such as "Deeds never require consideration" as " $\bar{r}$ " (which would read "It is not that deeds require consideration"), some of the emphasis of the original proposition is lost. However, this emphasis is not a matter of logic. Care is required, of course, in translating "never". In the above example, no particular harm was incurred in the translation, but where "never" has a time-reference, it is vital to ensure that this is not lost by expressing the corresponding proposition as a mere negation of a proposition in which "never" is excluded. If a proposition such as "Queen's Counsels are never ill-mannered" is felt to be inadequately expressed by "It is not that Queen's Counsels are ill-mannered", then it should be rendered for the purpose of symbolization as "There is no time at which a Queen's Counsel is ill-mannered", which is not a negated proposition. Negation may also arise in the use of popular opposites. Thus, in ordinary language, where a word such as "legal" is used, its opposite is often expressed as "illegal". Then, if " $Lx$ " is employed to represent "$x$ is legal", " $\bar{L}x$ " would represent "$x$ is illegal" (or "$x$ is not legal" or "It is not that $x$ is legal").

The conjunctor is usually expressed by the word "and". However, the use of "and" in logic does not always parallel its use in ordinary language. In logic, $K$ is employed to link propositions or predications whereas in ordinary language "and" may serve a different purpose. While "The judge and the prosecutor were angry" can be symbolized as $K\,j\,p$ (i.e. "The judge was angry and the prosecutor was angry"), one could not use a similar symbolization for "The judge and the prosecutor were acquainted", for here "and" does not link two simple propositions elliptically but expresses a certain relationship to be symbolized by the relational formula " $Auo$ ". It is essential to ensure that "and" occurring in ordinary language is not mechanically symbolized as $K$. This is of critical importance where "and" has a time-reference. In logic, $K\,p\,q$ is equivalent to $K\,q\,p$, but this is clearly not so in many instances of the use of "and" in ordinary language. It would be nonsense to treat "The victim made a statement and died" as equivalent to "The victim died and made a statement". In addition, "and" may have a causal import, which would not be captured by simply using $K$. "He drank brand X and became ill" implies that the drinking of brand X caused the illness; so it would be wrong to symbolize this in a manner which would treat it as if it were equivalent to the proposition "He became ill and drank brand X". In common usage, "and" links sentences that are related in content, whereas in logic, $K$ may conjoin any two propositions irrespective of their content and irrespective of how absurd such a combination may be. Although lawyers are rarely concerned with absurd conjunctions, it must be realized that such conjunctions are not excluded as a matter of logic. Apart from "and", ordinary language contains other expressions that signify the conjunctor. Thus expressions such as "but", "though", and "as well as" are frequently used to form conjunctions; when so used, they are naturally to be rendered by K.

The adjunctor is most commonly expressed by the word "or". Again, the use of "or" in logic is not necessarily parallel to its everyday use. What is called "adjunction" in this book is a kind of disjunction. A disjunction may be either strong or weak, the distinction being based on whether both disjuncts can co-exist or not. Thus "He is an adult or a minor" is a strong disjunction, since it is not possible to be both an adult and a minor. On the other hand, "To be eligible, one must be a graduate or a lecturer" is a weak disjunction (i.e. an adjunction), since one would still be eligible if one were both a graduate and a lecturer. It is solely for weak disjunction that A is used. A p q is taken to represent "p or q, possibly both"; thus it is equivalent to "and/or" as occurring in some legal expressions. Where the context indicates a strong disjunction (in this book called "contrabijunction"), the corresponding symbolization is $\bar{E}$ p q ("p or q, but not both", which can also be rendered as K A p q $\bar{K}$ p q). There are cases in which it is immaterial whether or not a strong disjunction is to be employed. If this is so, A will suffice; A will sometimes also do where it is uncertain whether a weak or a strong disjunction is intended. There are occasions on which "either ... or ..." does not express strong disjunction (i.e. contrabijunction) but is employed as a bracketing device in relation to weak disjunction (i.e. adjunction). Thus "He is incompetent and either deceitful or foolish" is not to be rendered as K i $\bar{E}$ e o but rather as K i A e o ; for "either" is used in this proposition to separate its adjunctive component from its conjunctive component.

The usual translations of the subjunctor as "if ... then ..." of the bijunctor as "if and only if ... then ...", and of the dejunctor as "only if ... then ..." represent only tolerable equivalents. In ordinary usage, there are a number of expressions which can be rendered by these three operators. Thus $C\,p\,q$ would represent any of the following: "if p, q", "provided that p, q", "p implies q", "p is a sufficient condition for q", and "p only if q". $E\,p\,q$ would represent any of the following: "exactly if p then q", "p if and only if q", "p coimplies q", and "p is a necessary and sufficient condition for q". $D\,p\,q$ would represent any of the following: "p if q", "only if p, q", "p provided that q", and "p is a necessary condition for q".

Part of the problems associated with the subjunctor, bijunctor, and dejunctor arise as a result of an indiscriminate use of "if ... then ...". One of the most frequent types of argument encountered in judicial reasoning is the apparent fallacy of denying the antecedent. For example, "If he started the fire then he is guilty of arson. He did not start the fire. Therefore he is not guilty of arson", which can easily be demonstrated to be an unsound argument. Yet, intuitively, the reasoning appears to be sound. When we begin to search for the reason of the invalidity of the conclusion, we find that "if" employed in the first premiss contains more than appears on the surface. Since presumably the defendent is not charged with any other offence, the first premiss should read "if and only if he started the fire then he is guilty of arson", whose symbolic expression is $E\,r\,g$. Using this as the first premiss, the conclusion is valid.

The word "unless" is generally regarded as equivalent to "if it is not that ... then ...". However, complications arise with the use of "unless" because in certain contexts implications may emerge which would not be expected from the mere tenor of the sentence used. For example, "Unless you are a member, you are excluded" would be represented as $C\,\bar{m}\,e$ ("If it is not that you are a member then you are excluded"). This statement does not imply $C\,m\,\bar{e}$ ("If you are a member then it is not that you are excluded"), since being a member is a necessary condition but may not be a sufficient condition for not being excluded. In contrast thereto, "Unless you forbid me, I shall come" could scarcely be treated as $C\bar{o}c$ , because there is an overwhelming implication to the effect of $Co\bar{c}$ ("If you forbid me then it is not that I shall come"). In such circumstances, the statement could be symbolized either as $KC\bar{o}cCo\bar{c}$ or as $E\bar{o}c$ . As always, it is not the words themselves but their contextual meaning which has to be represented.

The vagaries of ordinary language are such that an operator other than the normal one is appropriate. Thus it would be clearly incorrect to symbolize the sentence "Men and women are permitted to join" by the formula $\bigwedge_x CKMxWxPx$ , since this would read "For every $x$: if $x$ is a man and $x$ is a woman then $x$ is permitted to join". The word "and" cannot be represented by $K$ in this way. One correct symbolization would be $\bigwedge_x CAMxWxPx$ , which would read "For every $x$: if $x$ is a man or $x$ is a woman then $x$ is permitted to join". Another correct symbolization would be $\bigwedge_x KCMxPxCWxPx$ , which would read "For every $x$: if $x$ is a man then $x$ is permitted to join and if $x$ is a woman then $x$ is permitted to join".

Errors in symbolization may also occur if due regard is not paid to the construction of sentences. Ambiguities are liable to arise not only by virtue of the meanings of actual words used, but also by virtue of the particular placement of the words where the words themselves may have univocal meanings. If one knew nothing of the context, one would not know whether to symbolize "It is not the case that he was in London or in Paris" either as $\bar{A}oa$ or as $A\bar{o}a$ . In the former, the whole adjunction is negated whereas in the latter it is only the first adjunct that is negated. The intended meaning may be indicated by punctuation or by additional words. Thus, by adding a comma and "he was" it becomes clear that $A\bar{o}a$ is correct ("It is not the case that he was in London, or he was in Paris"). The insertion of a colon as in "It is not the case that: he was in London or in Paris" would show that $\bar{A}oa$ is meant. Similarly, "p or q and r" could mean either $KApqr$ or

ApKqr, whereas "p or q, and r" would indicate KApqr. As an ordinary language device of bracketing, the word "both" may be used here to establish the difference. Thus "p or both q and r" would indicate ApKqr.

Many other examples of this kind could be given with various combinations of the operators, particularly where a great number of these occur. Complex statutory provisions are the most likely source of the ambiguity in question. In most cases it is by the appropriate use of punctuation that one can tell which meaning is intended. Two standard constructions involving punctuation are "p, q, r and s" meaning KKKpqrs and "p, q and r, or s" meaning AKKpqrs.

## 2. *Problems with Predicators and Quantors*

It is by no means always easy to determine what is an appropriate predicator - whether one should symbolize by predicational formulae in as much detail as possible where simple symbolizations are available, and whether the same predicator may be employed for similar but not identical expressions used in the language to be symbolized. Frequently the tense used may have to be changed or the phrasing used may have to be modified in order to capture the intended meaning. Before one can use the same predicator for such an altered language, one must ensure that the same predicator applies.

A particular problem relating to predicators is that of identity and definite description. Thus, how is "Kurt Waldheim is the Secretary-General of the United Nations" to be symbolized? Intuitively, we know that something is amiss with *Sa*, where "*S*" stands for "is the Secretary-General of the United Nations" and "*a*" stands for "Kurt Waldheim". The reason that something strikes us as odd is that in other predications such as "*x* is a person", "*x* is a will", etc. there is no definite description signified by the predicator; there is only an indefinite description, viz. "... a person", "... a will", etc. in contrast to "... the Secretary-General of the United Nations". Yet it would make sense to have " *Sa* " mean "Kurt Waldheim is a Secretary-General of the United Nations" implying that there is more than one Secretary-General of the United Nations at present, which, of course, is a false statement (for the "troika proposal" was never acted on). It would be in any event unexceptionable to have " *Su* " stand for "U Thant was a Secretary-General of the United Nations", because he was not the only one.

In such definite description cases as the one above considered, the relator " *I* " can be employed to stand for "is identical to". Thus "Kurt Waldheim is the Secretary-General of the United Nations" can be symbolized as " *Iae* ", where " *a* " stands for "Kurt Waldheim" and " *e* " for "the Secretary-General of the United Nations". Thus " *Iae* " reads "Kurt Waldheim is identical to the Secretary-General of the United Nations". Similarly, "The accused is the man who was seen running from the scene of the crime" can be rendered by " *Iai* ", where " *a* " stands for "the accused" and " *i* " for "the man who was seen running from the scene of crime".

Where an identity relationship holds, the terms may replace one another wherever they occur. This is indicated by "I.R." ("Identity Relationship") in the deductions where a step of the procedure is based on this feature of the relationship.

There are occasions on which identity as a component of complex formulae enables us to symbolize sentences which would otherwise be difficult to express in the language of logic. Thus, how is "Kurt Waldheim is the sole Secretary-General of the United Nations" to be symbolized? Using " *a* " for "Kurt Waldheim", " *e* " for "Secretary-General of the United Nations", and " *I* " for "is identical to", the solution lies in the formula $\mathsf{K}\, Iae \underset{x}{\wedge}\mathsf{D}\, Ixa\; Ixe$ .

In regard to quantors, it is not invariably clear whether the universalizer (the U-quantor) or rather the particularizer (the P-quantor) applies in a given case. Language constructions are frequently irregular or idiomatic so that it is a matter of experience rather than a matter of mechanical application of rules to guide one to a correct symbolization. "No deeds require consideration" is clearly a universal statement; "Deeds never require consideration", "Deeds do not require consideration", and "A deed does not require consideration" are also universal statements, but they are less obviously so. In particular, in those examples where the subject appears in the singular, one must beware of treating it as belonging to a particular statement.

The formula of universalization " $\underset{x}{\wedge}$ " is usually expressed as "for all *x*", "for any *x*", and "for every *x*". Although the choice is largely stylistic, it is preferable to use "for every *x*", because "all" and "any" are particularly problem-ridden, as will appear in the sequel.

A common construction which can cause confusion is "All ... are not ...", such as "All graduates are not eligible". Does this mean that no graduates are eligible or some are eligible and some are not? One usually takes "All *x* are not *y*" to mean "Not all *x* are *y*" (i.e. some *x* are not *y*), but it is also possible for it to mean "No *x* are *y*". The context may reveal which of these meanings is the correct one.

That the word "any" has to be treated with caution appears from the following examples. In the statement "Whosoever abets the commission of any misdemeanor is liable to be punished as a principal offender", "any" should be symbolized by means of the universalizer thus $\underset{xy}{\wedge\wedge} C\, K\, K\, Px\, My$ - $Bxy\, Lx$ (where "$Px$" stands for "*x* is a person", "$My$" for "*y* is a misdemeanor", "$Bxy$" for "*x* abets the commission of *y*", and "$Lx$" for "*x* is liable to be punished as a principal offender"). This is so since it is any misdemeanor whatsoever that is referred to here. However, in the statement "If any tribunal upholds this decision then the whole legal profession will be dismayed", "any" does not indicate the universalizer; for symbolizing this sentence, the use of the particularizer is necessary since its meaning is "If there is a tribunal that upholds this decision ...". The requisite symbolization would be $C \bigvee_x K\ Tx\ Uxe\ p$ (where "$Tx$" stands for "$x$ is a tribunal", "$e$" for "this decision", "$Uxe$" for "$x$ upholds $e$", and "$p$" for "the whole legal profession will be dismayed"). To show the difficulties in this area, let us change the last example somewhat to read "If any tribunal upholds this decision then it is making an error". Again it is the universalizer that is necessary so that the correct symbolization would be $\bigwedge_x C\ K\ Tx\ Uxe\ Ex$ (where "$Ex$" stands for "$x$ is making an error"). This is by virtue of the fact that "it" in the statement refers back to "any tribunal".

Quantors may further be expressed by such words as "always" or "sometimes", the former indicating the universalizer and the latter indicating the particularizer. It is vital in such cases to ensure that the words used do not have a time-reference. For if they do, a quantor alone is not sufficient for rendering their meanings.

The formula of the particularizer "$\bigvee_x$" is briefly rendered by "for some $x$". It is often rendered also by "there is at least one $x$ such that" or by "at least one $x$ exists such that". When used as a technical logical word, "some" means "at least one, possibly all". This technical use of "some" is at variance with common usage, where the word frequently means "a few" and indicates more than one but not all.

Some problems relating to the use of the quantors arise within the framework of certain arguments. This is illustrated by the following example: "All who suffer from a defect of reason have a good defence. The accused suffers from a defect of reason. Therefore, the accused has a good defence". Let us use "$a$" for "the accused", "$Ex$" for "$x$ is a defect of reason", "$Syx$" for "$y$ suffers from $x$", and "$Dy$" for "$x$ has a good defence". It is clear that for the second premiss the particularizer will be necessary as it is not all defects of reason from which the accused must suffer but only some defect of reason or other. Accordingly, the second premiss would be symbolized as $\underset{x}{\vee}K\ Ex\ Sax$ (i.e. "For some *x*: *x* is a defect of reason and the accused suffers from *x*"). However, the first premiss is appropriately symbolized as follows by using the universalizer: $\underset{xy}{\wedge\wedge}C\ K\ Ex\ Syx\ Dy$ (i.e. "For every *x* and *y*: if *x* is a defect of reason and *y* suffers from *x* then *y* has a good defence"). The full argument can be symbolized as follows:

1. $\underset{xy}{\wedge\wedge}C\ K\ Ex\ Syx\ Dy$
2. $\underset{x}{\vee}K\ Ex\ Sax \qquad /\therefore\ \underline{Da}$

After a particular stigmication of the second premiss and a universal stigmication of the first premiss, the application of the *Modus Ponens* theorem yields the conclusion. Thus different quantors had to be used in connection with the phrase "suffer(s) from a defect of reason", but no problem arises by virtue of this symbolization. However, the symbolization given is not the only one available, for it would have been possible to represent the first premiss also by using the particularizer. Such a symbolization would be $\underset{y}{\wedge}C\ \underset{x}{\vee}K\ Ex\ Syx\ Dy$ (i.e. "For every *y*: if for some *x*: *x* is a defect of reason and *y* suffers from *x* then *y* has a good defence"). Note that when the particularizer is used in this symbolization, it has to be placed after the subjunctor in order to indicate the meaning of the given statement properly. It would be inadvisable to symbolize it as follows: $\underset{yx}{\wedge\vee}C\ K\ Ex\ Syx\ Dy$ (i.e. "For every *y* and for some *x*: if *x* is a defect of reason and *y* suffers from *x* then *y* has a good defence"). This might suggest that there was one and only one defect of reason the suffering of which would entitle an accused person to a good defence.

### 3. *Problems of Symbolizing Legal Language*

The language of legislation, of contracts, of wills, etc. raises additional problems of its logical organization emerging by virtue of the subject matter peculiar to it.

Basic problems will be examined in this section and specific problems in the next section.

Much is often made of the fact that propositional and predicational calculi deal with sentences in indicative mood whereas the language of law is characterized by expressions in imperative mood - it contains directives which stipulate, for example, that a person shall do something, may not do something, etc. However a closer examination of the language of law suggests that the task of its symbolization by forms of indicative logic is performable. Much of this language (e.g. "Whosoever does $y$ may do $z$") can be constructed in a rather simple subjunctive (conditional) form ("For every $x$ and for some $y$ and $z$: if $x$ does $y$ then $x$ may do $z$"). A part of the language of law is definitional normally expressed in indicative mood dispensing with deontic verbs (such as "shall" and "may") altogether. However, it cannot be ignored that these verbs do occur in it. When they occur, there are basically two different ways of handling them. One of these is to use deontic functors such as "obligatory" and "permissory" and deontic hypotacts such as "action" and "omission" and to give to the corresponding functions an extensional interpretation. The other way is merely to use ordinary predicational calculus and to treat the deontic verbs as relators. These verbs are understood as carrying the "directive force" in the expression of norms. Thus "All aliens shall register with the local authority" can be symbolized as $\underset{nr}{\wedge\vee} S^{c}nr$ (where "$n$" stands for "alien", "$r$" for "registering with the local authority", and "$S^{c}$" for "shall carry out"), which formula reads: "For every $n$ and for some $r$: $n$ shall carry out $r$".

In connection with this approach, the use of the word "may" raises a problem. In "You may take it", the meaning is that "You are permitted to take it". However, an unusual transformation takes place when "may" is followed by "not". Thus "You may not take it" is not usually understood to mean "You are permitted not to take it" but "You shall not take it" or "You are forbidden to take it". One must be constantly on guard to determine the actual meaning, since the most common meaning of "may not" is "shall not". Out of context, and sometimes even in context, "may not" could be quite ambiguous. Thus "He may not do it" can be taken to mean "It is forbidden for him to do it" or "Perhaps he will not do it". For indicating that a given deontic verb is negated without any further transformation, a hyphen can be used linking "not" with it (e.g. "may-not", "shall-not").

In the definition sections of statutes, the two most common forms encountered are "A means B" and "A includes B". These would be symbolized respectively as $\underset{x}{\wedge}E\ Ax\ Bx$ and $\underset{x}{\wedge}D\ Ax\ Bx$. Where the form "A includes B, C, and D" occurs, the appropriate symbolization would be $\underset{x}{\wedge}D\ Ax\ A\ A\ Bx\ Cx\ Dx$. Note that although "and" is used here, the adjunctor is the appropriate operator to be employed. One could scarcely be blamed for thinking that if "A includes B" is symbolized as $\underset{x}{\wedge}D\ Ax\ Bx$ then "A does not include B" would be symbolized as $\overline{\underset{x}{\wedge}}D\ Ax\ Bx$, which is equivalent to $\underset{x}{\vee}K\ \bar{A}x\ Bx$. But this is not what is meant. "A includes B and C, but does not include D" clearly means that Bs and Cs belong to A, but Ds belong to not-A. The appropriate symbolization would consequently be the following: $\underset{x}{\wedge}K\ D\ Ax\ A\ Bx\ Cx\ D\ \bar{A}x\ Dx$.

For symbolizing legal expressions, a glossary must be supplied. The glossary indicates first, how the predicators are to be used. A single set of dots indicates that the given predicator is monadic. Multiple sets of dots indicate that the given predicator is polyadic (i.e. a relator). Since legal expressions are often very complex, preferably synopic hypotacts with limited range of application are to be used, because in doing so, shorter formulae can be achieved. In order to place quantification coefficients conveniently, it is advisable to avoid high letters such as $k$ and $\ell$. Letters for symbols should be so selected that they would serve, if possible, as mnemonic labels for the expressions which they symbolize.

In the preliminary examples that follow, the language to be symbolized is given first, then a glossary of the symbols to be used, and then the symbolization followed by its approximate equivalent in ordinary language. These examples are all culled from typical definition sections of legal instruments.

"'Person' includes a company."

*P* : ... is a person

*C* : ... is a company

$\bigwedge_{n} \mathrm{D}\ Pn\ Cn$ :

For every *n*: only if *n* is a person then *n* is a company.

The same provision can be symbolized also by employing the subjunctor as follows:

$\bigwedge_{n} \mathrm{C}\ Cn\ Pn$ :

For every *n*: if *n* is a company then *n* is a person.

"'Minor' means a person who has not attained the age of 21 years."

*M* : ... is a minor

*P* : ... is a person

*T* : ... has attained the age of 21 years

$\bigwedge_{m} \mathrm{E}\ Mm\ \mathrm{K}\ Pm\ \bar{T}m$ :

For every *m*: *m* is a minor exactly if *m* is a person and it is not that *m* has attained the age of 21 years.

"'Consul' includes 'Consul-General', 'Vice-Consul', 'Pro-Consul', and 'Consular Agent'".

*C* : ... is a Consul

*G* : ... is a Consul-General

*V* : ... is a Vice-Consul

*P* : ... is a Pro-Consul

*A* : ... is a Consular Agent

$\bigwedge_{r} \mathrm{D}\ Cr\ \mathrm{A}\ \mathrm{A}\ \mathrm{A}\ Gr\ Vr\ Pr\ Ar$ :

For every *r*: only if *r* is a Consul then *r* is a Consul-General or *r* is a Vice-Consul or *r* is a Pro-Consul or *r* is a Consular Agent.

Note that "and" in the original is symbolized by using the adjunctor and thus becomes "or" in the translation into the language of logic. In the latter, "and" would not make sense. A symbolization using the conjunctor would be possible producing the following formula: $\bigwedge_r K\,K\,K\,C\,Gr\,Cr\,C\,Vr\,Cr\,C\,Pr\,Cr\,A\,Ar\,Cr$ , but this is cumbersome and inelegant.

"'Company' includes all bodies or associations corporate or incorporate but does not include partnerships."

*M* : ... is a company

*B* : ... is a body

*A* : ... is an association

*C* : ... is corporate

*I* : ... is incorporate

*P* : ... is partnership

$\bigwedge_s K\,D\,Ms\,K\,A\,Bs\,As\,A\,Cs\,Is\,D\,\bar{M}s\,Ps$ :

For every *s*: only if *s* is a company then *s* is a body or *s* is an association and *s* is corporate or *s* is incorporate and only if it is not that *s* is a company then *s* is a partnership.

The final unit of the above formula is an example of the phenomenon noted earlier, viz. in a legal definition "A does not include B" is not merely a negation of "A includes B". What is meant is that "A excludes B", that is, for example, "No companies are partnerships" (and vice versa). Thus, legally, "A does not include B" is not a contradictory but rather the contrary of "A includes B", whose proper symbolizations are $\bigwedge_x D\,\bar{A}x\,Bx$ , $\bigwedge_x D\,\bar{B}x\,Ax$ , $\bigwedge_x C\,Bx\,\bar{A}x$ , $\bigwedge_x C\,Ax\,\bar{B}x$ , or $\bigwedge_x \bar{K}\,Ax\,Bx$ (which are all equivalent).

"'Mortgage' includes any charge, lien or encumbrance to secure the repayment of money."

*M* : ... is a mortgage

*C* : ... is a charge

*L* : ... is a lien

*E* : ... is an encumbrance

*S* : ... is to secure the repayment of money

$\bigwedge_v D\,Mv\,K\,A\,A\,Cv\,Lv\,Ev\,Sv$ :

For every *v*: only if *v* is a mortgage then *v* is a charge or *v* is a lien or *v* is an encumbrance and *v* is to secure the repayment of money.

Note in particular that the phrase "to secure the repayment of money" is taken to qualify "charge", "lien" as well as "encumbrance". This type of construction, where a qualifying expression follows a number of preceding expressions, is particularly prone to ambiguity. It is always a matter of interpretation whether the final qualifying expression qualifies all the preceding expressions or merely the immediately preceding one. In the example above, it would be unreasonable to assume that "to secure the repayment of money" qualified only "encumbrance", and not "charge" and "lien".

Whether in definition sections or elsewhere, the same language can be translated into predicational formulae or into propositional formulae. Thus "Contracts of sale may be absolute or conditional" can be represented in the propositional form as $\mathsf{A}\, a\, c$ (where "a" stands for "Contracts of sale may be absolute" and "c" stands for "Contracts of sale may be conditional") or in the predicational form as $\bigwedge_{s} \mathsf{C}\, Ss\, \mathsf{A}\, As\, Cs$ (where "$Ss$" stands for "$s$ is a contract of sale", "$As$" for "$s$ is absolute" and "$Cs$" for "$s$ is conditional"). Which form to choose depends on the relevant context and on the purposes of the given symbolization. As a general rule, however, the simpler the symbolization the better, provided that it is adequate in view of the aims pursued. It is also possible to combine predicational and propositional formulae; for example, "If anyone saw the burglary and reported it to the police, the police would have rushed to the scene" could be rendered as follows: $\mathsf{C} \bigvee_{n} \mathsf{K}\, Snu\, Rnuo\, r$ (where "$u$" stands for "the burglary", "$o$" for "the police", "$Snu$" for "$n$ saw $u$", "$Rnuo$" for "$n$ reported $u$ to $o$", and "r" for "the police would have rushed to the scene"). The amount of the detail of such symbolization would be a matter of concrete decision depending on the nature of each particular problem.

### 4. *Examples of Symbolization from Various Legal Areas*

The point has now been reached where the logical equipment of this book can be put to the test of applying it to examples of legal language encountered daily in the work of the practitioner. The illustrations are taken from various sources to which he resorts in his professional activity. The translation of the formulae representing the selected provisions back to ordinary language should not cause any difficulty and it can henceforth be omitted to save space. Note that for reading the formulae aloud, the quantification coefficients can be called as "cap" (for " $\wedge$ ") and "wedge" (for " $\vee$ "). Thus the quantor " $\underset{r}{\wedge}$ " can be read as "cap-r".

*A Marriage Act Provision*

"A marriage may be solemnized on any day, at any time at any place"

Glossary: *r*: marriage; *v*: day; *m*: time; *c*: place; *O*: ... may be solemnized on ...; *A*: ... may be solemnized at ...

Formula: $\underset{rvmc}{\wedge\wedge\wedge\wedge} K\, K\, Orv\, Arm\, Arc$

*A Marriage Act Provision:*

"A person shall not solemnize, or purport to solemnize a marriage if he has reason to believe that there is a legal impediment to the marriage. Penalty: Five hundred dollars or imprisonment for six months."

Glossary: *r*: marriage; *s*: person; *S*: ... solemnizes ...; *P*: ... purports to solemnize ...; *R*: ... has reason to believe that there is a legal impediment to ...; *L*: ... is liable to penalty of ...; *o*: five hundred dollars; *i*: imprisonment for six months

Formula: $\underset{rs}{\wedge\wedge} C\, Rsr\, C\, A\, Ssr\, Psr\, \bar{E}\, Lso\, Lsi$

*A Crimes Act Provision:*

"1(a) Murder shall be taken to be committed where the act

of the accused or thing by him omitted to be done causing death was done or omitted with reckless indifference to human life, or with intent to kill of inflict grievous bodily harm upon some person or done in an attempt to commit during or immediately after the commission by the accused or some accomplice with him of an act obviously dangerous to life, or of a crime punishable by death or penal servitude for life.

(b) Every other punishable homicide shall be taken to be manslaughter."

"2(a) No act or omission which was not malicious of for which the accused had lawful cause or excuse shall be within this section.

(b) No punishment or forfeiture shall be incurred by any person who kills another by misfortune or in his own defence."

This is clearly not a simple example, and obviously the task of symbolizing is difficult here. When the symbolization of a lengthy provision is attempted, the best approach is to divide it and treat each component separately and ultimately link all the symbolized parts with appropriate operators. To make a legal provision amenable to expedient symbolization, it may be necessary to subject it to an interpretation. From this interpretation certain expressions result which the text of the provision itself does not contain. Thus in the following glossary "charged conduct" is introduced.

Glossary
for 1(a): $s$: accused; $g$: charged conduct; $p$: person; $c$: accomplice; $n$: act obviously dangerous to life; $r$: crime punishable by death; $m$: crime punishable by penal servitude for life; $M$: ... commits murder; $C$: ... was committed by ...; $O$: ... was omitted by ...; $D$: ... caused the death charged; $R^c$: ... committed ... with reckless indifference to the life of ...; $R^o$: ... omitted ... with reckless indifference to the life of ...; $I^c$: ... committed ... with intent

to kill ...; $I^o$: ... omitted ... with intent to kill ...; $G^c$: ... committed with intent to inflict grievous bodily harm on ...; $G^o$: ... omitted ... with intent to inflict grievous bodily harm on ...; $A$: ... did ... in an attempt to do ...; $U$: ... did ... during the commission of ...; $E$: ... did ... immediately after the commission of ...

Glossary for 1(b): $H$: ... is homicide; $P$: ... is punishable; $S$: ... is included in subsection 1(a); $L$: ... is manslaughter

Glossary for 2(a) $Z$: ... is malicious; $W$: ... had lawful cause for; $V$: ... had lawful excuse for ...; $T$: ... is within section 18

Glossary for 2(b): $K$: ... kills ... by misfortune; $N$: ... kills ... in his own defence; $J$: ... incurs punishment; $Q$: ... incurs forfeiture

Formulae

1(a): $\underset{s}{\wedge}\mathrm{D}\; Ms\; \underset{g}{\vee}\mathrm{K}\; \mathrm{K}\; \mathrm{A}\; Cgs\; Ogs\; Dg\; \mathrm{A}\; \underset{p}{\vee}\mathrm{A}\; \mathrm{A}\; \mathrm{A}\; R^c sgp\; R^o sgp\; \mathrm{A}\; \mathrm{A}\; I^c sgp$ -
$I^o sgp\; \mathrm{A}\; G^c sgp\; G^o sgp\; \underset{n}{\vee}\underset{r}{\vee}\underset{m}{\vee}\underset{c}{\wedge}\mathrm{A}\; \mathrm{A}\; \mathrm{A}\; \mathrm{A}\; Asgn\; Asgr\; Asgm\; \mathrm{A}\; \mathrm{A}\; Acgn$ -
$Acgr\; Acgm\; \mathrm{A}\; \mathrm{A}\; \mathrm{A}\; Usgn\; Usgr\; Usgm\; \mathrm{A}\; \mathrm{A}\; Ucgn\; Ucgr\; Ucgm\; \mathrm{A}\; \mathrm{A}\; \mathrm{A}$ -
$Esgn\; Esgr\; Esgm\; \mathrm{A}\; \mathrm{A}\; Ecgn\; Ecgr\; Ecgm$

1(b): $\underset{g}{\wedge}\mathrm{D}\; Lg\; \mathrm{K}\; \mathrm{K}\; Hg\; Pg\; \bar{S}g$

2(a): $\underset{g}{\wedge}\underset{s}{\wedge}\mathrm{D}\; \bar{T}g\; \mathrm{K}\; \mathrm{A}\; \mathrm{K}\; Cgs\; \bar{Z}g\; \mathrm{K}\; Ogs\; \bar{Z}g\; \mathrm{A}\; Wgs\; Vgs$

2(b): $\underset{s}{\wedge}\underset{p}{\wedge}\mathrm{D}\; \mathrm{K}\; Js\; Gs\; \mathrm{A}\; Ksp\; Nsp$

Note that in 2(a) "lawful" is understood as qualifying both "cause" and "excuse". Although clearcut in the present context, in many instances such qualification is not a matter of course and it is not certain whether or not the qualification is distributed over subsequent terms.

*A Treaty Provision:*

"Each Member Country may cease being a party to one or more of the Agreements, under the conditions laid down in Article 12."

Glossary: *n*: country; *r*: agreement; *u*: The Universal Postal Union; *M*: ... is a member of ...; *C*: ... may cease being a party to ...; w: The conditions laid down in Article 12 are followed

Formula: $\wedge\!\wedge_{nr} \mathrm{D}\ \mathrm{C}\ \mathrm{w}\ Cnr\ Mnu$

Note the use of " w ", which signifies an unanalyzed statement within a predicational framework. The statement could have been expressed in predicational (instead of propositional) form, but it is often more convenient to leave the statement predicationally unarticulated when its internal structure is unrelated to the rest of the context.

*A Common Clause in Contracts for the Sale of Land:*

"The purchaser shall accept all abstracted deeds as conclusive evidence of everything therein stated or assumed."

Glossary: *c*: deed; *r*: matter; *u*: the purchaser; *B*: ... is abstracted; *T*: ... shall accept ... as conclusive evidence of ...; *R*: ... is recited in ...; *S*: ... is stated in ...; *M*: ... is assumed in ...

Formula: $\wedge\!\wedge_{cr} \mathrm{D}\ Tucr\ \mathrm{K}\ Bc\ \mathrm{A}\ \mathrm{A}\ Rrc\ Src\ Mrc$

Note that "matter" is used in the glossary for "-thing" in "everything". Note also that "the purchaser" is not rendered by synopic but by a stigmic hypotact, because in a particular contract it designates an individual entity.

*A Mortgage Provision:*

"The statutory powers of leasing shall be exercisable only by the borrower personally and shall not extend to persons claiming under him."

Glossary: *s*: statutory power of leasing; *p*: person claiming under the borrower; *o*: the borrower; *M*: ... may exercise ...; *T*: extends to ...; *L*: ... claims ...; *I*: ... is identical to ...

Formula: $\wedge\!\wedge_{sp} \mathrm{K}\ Mos\ \mathrm{K}\ \mathrm{C}\ \bar{I}po\ \bar{M}ps\ \mathrm{C}\ Lp\ \bar{T}sp$

A point of interest in this example is the varying use of "shall". In "shall be exercisable", "shall" is not a duty concept and the phrase could be replaced by "are exercisable" or "may be exercised". In "shall not extend", "shall" carries no directive force and could simply be replaced by "do".

*A Common Provision in Wills:*

"I devise and bequeath all the residue of my property to A."

Glossary: *r*: property; *s*: person (i.e. anyone); *i*: I (i.e. the testator); *a*: A; *D*: ... devises ... to ...; *B*: ... bequeaths ... to ...; *P*: ... is property of ...

Formula: $\underset{r}{\wedge}\mathrm{C}\ \mathrm{K}\ Pri\ \underset{s}{\bar{\vee}}\mathrm{A}\ \mathrm{K}\ Isa\ Dirs\ Birs\ \mathrm{K}\ Dira\ Bira$

In the above formula there appears a negated particularizer. It would have been possible to express the relevant thought by means of "... $\underset{s}{\wedge}\bar{\mathrm{A}}$ ...", however, this symbolization when translated back into ordinary language would yield a prose which is less straightforward than the one which the given symbolization yields. The negated particularizer reads as "It is not that for some *x*".

*R. v. Lumley (1911) 22 Cox C.C. 635:*

"If a doctor carries out an illegal operation on a woman and causes her death thereby, he is guilty of manslaughter unless he intended or foresaw the woman's death as a probable consequence of his act in which case he is guilty of murder."

Glossary: *c*: doctor; *r*: operation; *w*: woman; *R*: ... carries out ... on ...; *L*: ... is legal; *D*: ... causes the death of ... by ...; *S*: ... is guilty of manslaughter; *M*: ... is guilty of murder; *I*: ... intended the death of ... as a probable consequence of his act; *F*: ... foresaw the death of ... as a probable consequence of his act

Formula: $\underset{rcw}{\wedge\wedge\wedge}\mathrm{C}\ \mathrm{K}\ \bar{L}r\ \mathrm{K}\ Rcrw\ Dcwr\ \mathrm{K}\ \mathrm{D}\ Sc\ \bar{\mathrm{A}}\ Icw\ Fcw\ \mathrm{D}\ Mc\ \mathrm{A}\ Icw\ Fcw$

## II. Logical Testing of Judicial Reasoning

### 1. *Applications of the Short-cut Tabular Method*

This chapter examines arguments of judicial reasoning presented either by counsel or by judges. Examples will be given for the application of the three most efficient methods of logical testing: the short-cut tabular method, the direct proof method, and the counter-formula method. Since the indirect proof method has the same basis as the counter-formula method, but is less efficient and comprehensive than the latter, no examples will be given for its application. The conditional proof method does not seem to have any advantage where the deductive instrumentarium is adequate in respect of rules of derivation or theorems. Since the direct proof and the counter-formula methods as presented in this book have such instrumentariums, it would be unnecessary to resort to the conditional proof method in the following.

In each example throughout the chapter, the facts of a case are presented first, then the text of its argument, then the logical structure of the argument in ordinary language, then a glossary for the logically structured argument, and finally the argument in symbolized form together with the demonstration of the validity or invalidity, solidity or insolidity of its conclusion. Wherever feasible, the logical structure of arguments will be presented in an abbreviated (elliptical) language.

Within the confines of a single chapter, it is not possible, of course, to present the full text of any particular case or even a complete judgment, nor is it possible to provide as many illustrations as may be desired. Nevertheless, the examples chosen supply the relevant parts of a representative cross-section and range from the not too difficult to some that are rather complex. In choosing examples for logical testing, it can be seen that judicial statements frequently contain extraneous material that is not required to establish logically the claimed conclusion, yet which judges seem to have felt necessary for substantiating or bolstering their reasoning. Such material is superfluous for deductive reasoning but may be significant for zetetic arguments, especially for those by which justification of value judgments is aspired. These arguments are an important subject of the legal method, but they are beyond the scope of this book.

After these preliminaries, the application of the STM will now be illustrated in two cases. In the presentation of the facts of the case and of the text of the argument of the first case, two expressions occur which are not commonly used in the United States. Their American equivalents will be supplied in square brackets where they first occur.

Musgrove *v.* Pandelis
(1919) 2 K.B. 43
Legal Area: Torts

*The Facts of the Case:*

A motor car [automobile] had been brought into a garage with a full petrol [gas] tank. The tank had caught fire and the ignition had not been switched off. In consequence the fire spread and caused damage to the plaintiff's property.

*The Text of the Argument:*

Bankes, L.J.: A man was liable at common law for damage done by fire originating on his own property (1) for the mere escape of the fire, (2) if the fire was caused by the negligence of himself or his servants or by his own wilful act, (3) upon the principle in Rylands *v.* Fletcher ... The question then is whether this motor car with its petrol tank full was a dangerous thing to bring into the garage within the principle in Rylands *v.* Fletcher. ... I agree with Lush, J. that this motor car was dangerous within this principle. The defendant brought or caused it to be brought upon his premises and he is responsible for the fire which resulted and is not within the protection of the statute.

*The Logical Structure of the Argument:*

If there is the mere escape of the fire or the fire was caused by the defendant's or his servants' negligence or by his own wilful act, or the principle in Rylands *v*. Fletcher applies, then the defendant is liable for damage done by fire originating on his own property. If the defendant's act was dangerous then the principle in Rylands *v*. Fletcher applies. If the defendant brought or caused to be brought the motor car into the garage then the defendant's act was dangerous. The defendant brought or caused to be brought the car into the garage. Therefore, the defendant is liable.

For many purposes of judicial reasoning, propositional calculus is a blunt tool; however, in the present case it is adequate.

*Glossary:*

e : There is the mere escape of fire

a : The fire was caused by the defendant's own or his servants' negligence or by his own wilful act

i : The principle in Rylands *v*. Fletcher applies

n : The defendant's act was dangerous

r : The defendant brought or caused to be brought the motor car into the garage

m : The defendant is liable for the damage done by the fire

*The Argument in the Statement Form:*

C / K K K C A A e a i m C n i C r n r /.'. m

*Solidity Proof:*

In order to determine by the STM whether the conclusion of the above argument is solid, the formula which expresses its derivation base is to be subjected to a dyslogy test. If this formula proves to be not dyslogous, the conclusion of the argument is solid.

| K | K | K | C | A | A | e | a | i | m | C | n | i | C | r | n | r |
|---|---|---|---|---|---|---|---|---|---|---|---|---|---|---|---|---|
| + | + | + | + | + | + | + | + | + | + | + | + | + | + | + | + | + |
| 1 | 2 | 3 | 4 | 10 | 12 | 13 | 14 | 9 | 11 | 4 | 7 | 8 | 3 | 5 | 6 | 2 |

The above test did not produce any inconsistency in the ascription of the signs. Therefore, the tested formula is not a dyslogy and the conclusion of the above argument is solid. Note that Steps 12, 13, and 14 did not involve compulsory but only possible ascriptions.

*Validity Proof:*

In order to determine by the STM whether the conclusion of the above argument is valid, the formula which expresses this argument is to be subjected to a tautology test. If the formula proves to be tautologous, the conclusion of the argument is valid:

| C | K | K | K | C | A | A | a | e | i | m | C | n | i | C | r | n | r | m |
|---|---|---|---|---|---|---|---|---|---|---|---|---|---|---|---|---|---|---|
| − | + | + | + | + | − | − | | | − | − | + | − | − | + | − | − | + | − |
| 1 | 2 | 3 | 4 | 5 | 7 | 8 | | | 8 | 6 | 5 | 10 | 9 | 4 | 12 | 11 | 3 | 2 |

Step 12 produced an inconsistency, because the sign ascribed to *r* by Step 3 is plus whereas the sign ascribed to *r* by Step 12 is minus. Therefore, the tested formula is a tautology and the conclusion of the above argument is valid.

Broom *v*. Morgan
(1953) 1 Q.B. 597
Legal Area: Torts

*The Facts of the Case:*

A husband and his wife were employed on the same premises . The husband negligently injured the wife. The wife sued the employer.

*The Text of the Argument (by Counsel for the Defendant):*

Vicarious liability and initial liability are two different branches of liability. If it is merely vicarious liability, a pre-condition is that there must be liability on the part of the actor - in this case the husband - who must have been under a duty not to act negligently *quoad* his wife. A husband owes no duty, imposed and recognized by law, not to cause injury to his wife by negligence. Even if he hit her on the head she would have no remedy in tort against him, though she could charge him with assault. There being no cause of action known to the law, there is no tort. "Tort" signifies an actionable wrong. What the husband did *quoad* his wife was not an actionable wrong and therefore there was nothing for which the employer was liable at law.

*The Logical Structure of the Argument:*

For every *x*: if *x* commits a tort then *x* commits an actionable wrong. It is not that the husband commits an actionable wrong. If it is not that the husband is liable then it is not that the employer is liable. It is not that the employer is liable.

There is a further unexpressed premiss involved in this argument, namely that one is liable if and only if one commits a tort. This is to be added as an additional premiss; its formula will be placed between square brackets to indicate the enthymematic character which its absence in counsel's pleading lends to the argument. Note that the argument requires only one synopic hypotact; therefore it can be expressed in the abbreviated notation of predicational calculus.

*Glossary:*

*T* : ... commits a tort

*W* : ... commits an actionable wrong

*L* : ... is liable

*u* : the husband

*e* : the employer

*The Argument in the Statement Form:*

$$\wedge C\,/\,K\,K\,K\,C\;T\;W\;\bar{W}u\;C\;\bar{L}u\;\bar{L}e\;[\;E\;L\;T\;]\;/\,.\!\cdot\!.\;\bar{L}e$$

After the synopic hypotacts in the derivation base have been subjected to the universal stigmication, the argument can be expressed as follows:

$$C\,/\,K\,K\,K\,C\;Tu\;Wu\;\bar{W}u\;C\;\bar{L}u\;\bar{L}e\;[\;E\;Lu\;Tu\;]\;/\,.\!\cdot\!.\;\bar{L}e$$

In order to determine the solidity of the conclusion of this argument, the derivation base of the argument will be subjected to a dyslogy test. In order to determine the validity of the conclusion of this argument, its formula will be subjected to a tautology test. The predications contained in the formulae to be tested will be treated as if they were propositions.

*Solidity Proof:*

$$\begin{array}{ccccccccccccccc} K & K & K & C & Tu & Wu & \overline{Wu} & C & \overline{Lu} & \overline{Le} & [ & E & Lu & Tu & ] \\ + & + & + & + & - & - & + & + & + & + & & + & - & - & \\ 1 & 2 & 3 & 4 & 6 & 5 & 4 & 3 & 9 & 10 & & 2 & 8 & 7 & \end{array}$$

The above test did not produce any inconsistency in the ascription of the signs. Therefore, the tested formula is not a dyslogy and the conclusion of the argument tested is solid. Note that all steps are compulsory in this test.

*Validity Proof:*

$$\begin{array}{ccccccccccccccccc} C & K & K & K & C & Tu & Wu & \overline{Wu} & C & \overline{Lu} & \overline{Le} & [ & E & Lu & Tu & ] & \overline{Le} \\ - & + & + & + & + & - & - & + & + & + & \boxed{+} & & + & - & - & & \boxed{-} \\ 1 & 2 & 3 & 4 & 5 & 7 & 6 & 5 & 4 & 10 & \boxed{11} & & 3 & 9 & 8 & & \boxed{2} \end{array}$$

Step 11 brings out an inconsistency in relation to the sign already ascribed to $\overline{Le}$ by Step 2. Therefore, the tested formula is a tautology and the conclusion of the argument tested is valid.

## 2. *Applications of the Direct Proof Method*

Where the short-cut tabular method proves to be too cumbrous, the direct proof method may furnish an expedient procedure for proving the validity of the conclusion of a judicial argument. However, this method does not constitute a logical decision-procedure and has therefore only a limited application in the logical testing of judicial reasoning. Moreover, it is not automatic (while the tabular methods are) and thus it depends on the ingenuity and insight of those who seek to establish the logical soundness of an argument.

R. *v.* Ashwell
(1885) 16 Q.B.D. 190
Legal Area: Criminal Law

*The Facts of the Case:*

Ashwell, the accused, requested the loan of a shilling and received a coin which he and the lender believed to be a shilling. Ashwell later discovered that it was a sovereign and decided to convert it to his own use. He was convicted of larceny.

*The Text of the Argument:*

Stephens, J. (on appeal): ... The rule that in every theft there must be a felonious taking, or in other words a trespass, and that a fraudulent conversion after an innocent taking is not theft is laid down by every text-writer who has dealt with the subject ... and has been recognized by many statutes which make exceptions to it in the case of embezzlement by servants, misappropriation by agents and especially in the case of larceny by bailees ... The application of this principle to the present case appears to me direct and obvious. Ashwell received the sovereign innocently, though he dealt with it fraudulently an hour afterwards when he became aware of its value. The inference that he committed no felony at common law appears to me to follow of necessity.

In tackling judicial arguments, it is often necessary to prune the verbiage so as to bring out the gist of the logical aspect of the argument by eliminating expressions which are inessential from the logical point of view. When this is done with respect to the above text, the argument would consist of the following statements:

A felonious taking is a necessary condition for larceny. A felonious taking is equivalent to a trespass. If the taking is innocent then a later fraudulent conversion does not amount to larceny except for embezzlement by servants, misappropriation by agents, and bailees' larceny. Ashwell's taking of the sovereign was innocent. He later committed a fraudulent conversion. Therefore, he is not guilty of larceny.

*The Logical Structure of the Argument:*

For every *m*: if *m* commits larceny then for some *n*: *m* takes *n* and *m* acts feloniously. For every *m*: exactly if for some *n*: *m* takes *n* and *m* acts feloniously then *m* commits a trespass. For every *m*: if for some *n*: *m* takes *n* and *m* acts innocently and *m* fraudulently converts *n* to his use subsequent to the original taking and neither *m* is a servant and *m* commits embezzlement or *m* is an agent and *m* commits misappropriation nor *m* commits a bailees' larceny then it is not that *m* commits larceny. Ashwell takes the sovereign and Ashwell is innocent. Ashwell fraudulently converts the sovereign to his own use subsequent to the original taking. Therefore, it is not that Ashwell is guilty of larceny.

This argument contains at least one suppressed premiss, which can be expressed as follows:

For every *m* : if *m* acts feloniously then it is not that *m* acts innocently.

*Glossary:*

*B* : ... commits a bailees' larceny

*F* : ... acts feloniously

*G* : ... is an agent

*I* : ... acts innocently

*L* : ... commits larceny

*M* : ... commits misappropriation

*P* : ... commits a trespass

*S* : ... is a servant

*T* : ... takes ...

*V* : ... fraudulently converts ... to his own use subsequent to the original taking

*Z* : ... commits embezzlement

*a* : Ashwell

*o* : the sovereign

*Validity Proofs:*

I:

1. $\bigwedge_m \mathrm{C}\ Lm\ \bigvee_n \mathrm{K}\ Tmn\ Fm$
2. $\bigwedge_m \mathrm{E}\ \bigvee_n \mathrm{K}\ Tmn\ Fm\ Pm$
3. $\bigwedge_m \mathrm{C}\ \mathrm{K}\ \bigvee_n \mathrm{K}\ \mathrm{K}\ Tmn\ Im\ Vmn\ \bar{\mathrm{A}}\ \mathrm{A}\ \mathrm{K}\ Sm\ Zm\ \mathrm{K}\ Gm\ Mm\ Bm\ \bar{L}m$
4. $\mathrm{K}\ Tao\ Ia$
5. $Vao$

[ 6. $\bigwedge_m \mathrm{C}\ Fm\ \bar{I}m$ ] /∴ $\bar{L}a$

7. $Ia$ 4, C.E.

| | | |
|---|---|---|
| 8. | $C\ Fa\ \bar{I}a$ | 6, U.T. |
| 9. | $\bar{F}a$ | 8,7, M.T. |
| 10. | $C\ La\ \underset{n}{\vee}K\ Tan\ Fa$ | 1, U.T. |
| 11. | $A\ \bar{L}a\ \underset{n}{\vee}K\ Tan\ Fa$ | 10, Dual. |
| 12. | $\underset{n}{\vee}A\ \bar{L}a\ K\ Tan\ Fa$ | 11, Q.L. |
| 13. | $A\ \bar{L}a\ K\ Tae\ Fa$ | 12, P.T. |
| 14. | $A\ \bar{F}a\ \bar{T}ae$ | 9, Add. |
| 15. | $A\ \bar{T}ae\ \bar{F}a$ | 14, Comm. |
| 16. | $\bar{K}\ Tae\ Fa$ | 15, Dual., D.N. |
| 17. | $\bar{L}a$ | 13,16, A.E. |

Note that in this proof the only premisses used were 1, 4, and the suppressed premiss 6. In other words, for the purpose of establishing the sought conclusion, the judge could have discarded Premisses 2, 3, and 5. However, the adoption of the particular enthymeme above is too facile an approach since it does not take into account the possibility of an innocent taking becoming larceny in the case of embezzlement by servants, misappropriation by agents, and larceny by bailees. In view of these, Premiss 6 is not adequate for the argument and a preferable proof would include three suppressed premisses, viz.

> It is not that Ashwell is a servant and Ashwell commits embezzlement. It is not that Ashwell is an agent and Ashwell commits misappropriation. It is not that Ashwell commits bailees' larceny.

II: 1, 2, 3, 4, and 5 as in Proof I above

| | | |
|---|---|---|
| [ 6. | $\bar{K}\ Sa\ Za$ ] | |
| [ 7. | $\bar{K}\ Ga\ Ma$ ] | |
| [ 8. | $\bar{B}a$ ] | /∴ $\bar{L}a$ |
| 9. | $K\ K\ \bar{K}\ Sa\ Za\ \bar{K}\ Ga\ Ma\ \bar{B}a$ | 6,7,8, R.C. |
| 10. | $K\ \bar{A}\ K\ Sa\ Za\ K\ Ga\ Ma\ \bar{B}a$ | 9, Dual., D.N. |
| 11. | $\bar{A}\ A\ K\ Sa\ Za\ K\ Ga\ Ma\ Ba$ | 10, Dual., D.N. |

12. $C\,K\,\overset{v}{\underset{n}{}}K\,K\,\mathit{Tan}\,\mathit{Ia}\,\mathit{Van}\,\bar{A}$ - $\quad$ 3, U.T.
$A\,K\,\mathit{Sa}\,\mathit{Za}\,K\,\mathit{Ga}\,\mathit{Ma}\,\mathit{Ba}\,\bar{\mathit{La}}$

13. $K\,K\,\mathit{Tao}\,\mathit{Ia}\,\mathit{Vao}$ $\quad$ 4,5, R.C.

14. $vK\,K\,\mathit{Tan}\,\mathit{Ia}\,\mathit{Van}$ $\quad$ 13, P.Y.

15. $K\,vK\,K\,\mathit{Tan}\,\mathit{Ia}\,\mathit{Van}\,\bar{A}\,A$ - $\quad$ 14,11, R.C.
$K\,\mathit{Sa}\,\mathit{Za}\,K\,\mathit{Ga}\,\mathit{Ma}\,\mathit{Ba}$

16. $\bar{\mathit{La}}$ $\quad$ 12,15, M.P.

Note that in this proof, Premisses 1 and 2 were not used, while in neither proof was Premiss 2 used. Such redundant premisses detract from logical elegance of arguments; in judicial reasoning they are nevertheless employed in order to add force of persuasion to forensic argumentation.

Shirlaw *v.* Southern Foundries
(1939) 2 K.B. 206
Legal Area: Contract Law

*The Facts of the Case:*

The plaintiff sued the defendant for the wrongful repudiation of an agreement appointing him managing director. The question arose whether there was an implied provision in the agreement that the company should not terminate Shirlaw's directorship which would thereby terminate his position as managing director.

*The Text of the Argument:*

McKinnon, L.J.: For my part, I think that there is a test that may be at least as useful as such generalities. If I may quote from an essay which I wrote some years ago, I then said: "*Prima facie* that which in any contract is left implied and need not be expressed is something so obvious that it goes without saying; so that if, while the parties were making their bargain, an officious bystander were to suggest some express provision for it in their agreement, they would testily suppress him with a common 'Oh, of course!'". At least it is true, I think, if a term were never implied by a judge unless it could pass that test, he could

> not be held to be wrong. Applying that in this case, I ask myself what would have happened if, when their contract had been drafted and was awaiting signature, a third party reading the draft had said, "Would it not be well to put in a provision that the company shall not exercise or create any right to remove Mr. Shirlaw from his directorship, and he have no right to resign his directorship?". I am satisfied that they would both have assented to this as implied and agreed to its expression for greater security ...

Reducing the judge's rather verbose reasoning to the bare essentials of logical argument, we have:

> A provision is implied in a contract if it is so obvious that it goes without saying. It has the required obvious nature if the parties would readily assent to it if it is brought to their attention before the contract is completed. Applying this to the present case, if before the contract was completed, the provision that the company should not exercise or create any right to remove Mr. Shirlaw from his directorship and that he should have no right to resign his directorship had been brought to the attention of the parties then they would have readily assented to them. Hence this provision is implied in the contract.

*The Logical Structure of the Argument:*

> For every *r* (i.e. obvious provision) and *c* (i.e. contract): *r* is implied in *c* if *r* is so obvious that it goes without saying. For every *r*, every *p* (contractual party), and every *c*: *r* is so obvious that it goes without saying if *p* would readily assent to *r* if *p* is a party to *c* if *r* is brought to the attention of *p* before *c* is completed. If the provision that the company should not exercise or create any right to remove Mr. Shirlaw from his directorship and that he should have no right to resign his directorship had been brought to the attention of the parties before the contract was completed then the parties would have readily

assented to the provision. Therefore, the provision is implied in the contract.

The argument contains also the following suppressed premiss:

For every *p*, every *r*, and every *c*: *p* would readily assent to *r* if *p* is a party to *c* if *r* is brought to the attention of *p* before *c* is completed.

*Glossary:*

*I* : ... is implied in ...

*O* : ... is so obvious that it goes without saying

*B* : ... is brought to the attention of ... before ... is completed

*R* : ... is a party of ...

*S* : ... would readily assent to ...

*a* : the contractual parties in the present case

*e* : the provision that the company should not exercise or create any right to remove Mr. Shirlaw from his directorship and that he should have no right to resign

*o* : the contract in the present case

*Validity Proof:*

1. $\bigwedge\bigwedge_{rc} D \; Irc \; Or$
2. $\bigwedge\bigwedge\bigwedge_{rpc} D \; Or \; K \; Spr \; K \; Rpc \; Brpc$
3. $C \; Beao \; Sae$

[ 4. $\bigwedge\bigwedge\bigwedge_{prc} K \; Spr \; K \; Rpc \; Brpc$ ] $/ \therefore$ $\underline{Ieo}$

5. $D \; Ieo \; Oe$ — 1, U.T.
6. $A \; Ieo \; \bar{O}e$ — 5, Dual.
7. $D \; Oe \; K \; Sae \; K \; Rao \; Beao$ — 2, U.T.
8. $A \; Oe \; \bar{K} \; Sae \; K \; Rao \; Beao$ — 7, Dual.
9. $K \; Sae \; K \; Rao \; Beao$ — 4, U.T.
10. $Oe$ — 8,9, A.E.
11. $Ieo$ — 6,10, A.E.

It was possible here to prove the validity of the conclusion without making use of Premiss 3.

### 3. *Applications of the Counter-formula Method*

In contrast to the direct proof method, not only the validity but also the invalidity of conclusions can be proved by the counter-formula method. In the present section, only validity proofs are provided for legal conclusions (together with their solidity proofs). In the final section of this chapter, the CFM will be employed to prove also the invalidity of conclusions of legal arguments.

R. *v*. Larkin
(1943) 1 All E.R. 217
Legal Area: Criminal Law

*The Facts of the Case:*

The deceased, a woman with whom the accused had been living, was mortally wounded in the throat by a razor held by the accused. The accused stated that he had produced the razor to frighten another man with whom the deceased had been associating and the deceased, groggy with drink, had blundered against the razor.

*The Text of the Argument:*

Humphries, J.: Where the act which a person is engaged in performing is unlawful, then, if at the same time it is a dangerous act, that is, an act which is likely to injure another person, and quite inadvertently he causes the death of that person by that act, then he is guilty of manslaughter ...

*The Logical Structure of the Argument:*

If the accused's act is unlawful and dangerous and inadvertently causes the death of a bystander then the accused is guilty of manslaughter. If the accused's act is likely to injure someone then it is dangerous. If the accused brandished a razor to frighten someone then his act is unlawful and is likely to injure someone. The accused brandished a razor to frighten someone and inadvertently caused the death of a bystander. Therefore, the accused is guilty of manslaughter.

*Glossary:*

u : The accused's act is unlawful

a : The accused's act is dangerous

o : The accused's act is likely to injure someone

s : The accused's act inadvertently caused the death of a bystander

r : The accused brandished a razor to frighten someone

m : The accused is guilty of manslaughter

***Consolidated Solidity and Validity Proof:***

| | | |
|---|---|---|
| 1. | CKKuasm | |
| 2. | Coa | |
| 3. | CrKuo | |
| 4. | Krs | /∴ m |
| 5. | A$\bar{K}$Kuasm | 1, S.Dual. |
| 6. | AA$\bar{K}$ua$\bar{s}$m | 5, CC.Dual. |
| 7. | AAA$\bar{u}\bar{a}\bar{s}$m | 6, CC.Dual |
| 8. | A$\bar{o}$a | 2, S.Dual. |
| 9. | A$\bar{r}$Kuo | 3, S.Dual. |
| 10. | r , s | 4, K.E. |
| 11. | Kuo | 9,10, A.E. |
| 12. | u , o | 11, K.E. |
| 13. | a | 8,12, A.E. |
| 14. | AA$\bar{u}\bar{a}$m | 7,10, A.E. |
| 15. | A$\bar{a}$m | 14,12, A.E. |
| 16. | m | 15,13, A.E. |

Solid: F-CF unattainable

| | | |
|---|---|---|
| 17. | $\bar{m}$ | CFC |

Valid: 16,17: F-CF

Note that in the above consolidated procedure there was no need to treat the entry representing the CFC as following the last premiss. Thus it could be numbered as "17".

Mortensen *v.* Peters
High Court of Justiciary of Scotland
(1906) 8 Session Cases, 5th Series, 93

*The Facts of the Case:*

The appellant being a foreign subject, and master of a vessel registered in a foreign country, exercised the method of fishing known as otter-trawling at a point within the Moray Firth, more than three miles from the shore, but to the west of a line drawn from Duncansby Head ... that being thereafter found within British territory ..., he was summoned to the Sheriff at Dornoch to answer to a complaint against him for having contravened the 7th section of the Herring Fishery Board, thereunder made, and was convicted ...

*The Text of the Argument* (as stated by the Lord Justice-General)*:*

The Counsel for the Appellant: ... statutes creating offences must be presumed to apply only (1) to British subjects; and (2) to foreign subjects in British territory; and short of express enactment their application should not be further extended. The appellant is not a British subject, which excludes (1); and ... the *locus delicti*, being in the sea beyond the three-mile limit, was not within British territory; ... consequently the appellant was not included in the prohibition of the statute.

*The Logical Structure of the Argument:*

For every *j* (i.e. norm-subject) and every *s* (i.e. statute): if *j* is included in the prohibition of *s* then *j* is a British subject or *j* is a foreign subject in British territory or *s* can be extended in its application. The appellant is neither a British subject nor is the appellant a foreign subject in British territory. Therefore, it is not that the appellant is included in the prohibition of the relevant statute.

The argument contains also the following suppressed premiss:

It is not that the relevant statute can be extended in its application.

*Glossary:*

*I* : ... is included in the prohibition of ...

*B* : ... is a British subject

*F* : ... is a foreign subject in British territory

*E* : ... can be extended in its application

*a* : the appellant

*u* : the relevant statute

*Consolidated Solidity and Validity Proof:*

1. $\wedge_{j}\wedge_{s} C\, Ijs\, A\, A\, Bj\, Fj\, Es$
2. $\bar{A}\, Ba\, Fa$

[ 3. $\bar{E}u$ ] /∴ $\bar{I}au$

4. $C\, Iau\, A\, A\, Ba\, Fa\, Eu$ — 1, U.T.
5. $A\, \bar{I}au\, A\, A\, Ba\, Fa\, Eu$ — 4, S.Dual.
6. $A\, \bar{I}au\, A\, Ba\, Fa$ — 5,3, A.E.
7. $\bar{I}au$ — 6,2, A.E.

Solid: F-CF unattainable

8. $Iau$ — CFC

Valid: 7,8: F-CF

Note that in the above consolidated procedure, too, there was no need to treat the entry representing the CFC as following the last premiss. This is because an occasion of applying the rule of P.T. could not arise here.

### 4. *Invalidity and Insolidity in Legal Reasoning*

If the legal arguments were to be regarded as consisting exclusively of the expressions actually used by legal reasoners, it would prove that a great many arguments which occur in the world of law are formally unsound. Legal arguments encountered in lawyers' practical activities require expedient handling; they are therefore abbreviated (enthymematic) - those premisses which are self-understood or readily available are suppressed. If these are discarded, the claimed conclusions may prove to be invalid.

If self-understood or readily available premisses are also taken into account, it is not a common occurrence to come across examples of formal invalidity in legal reasoning, for counsel and judges are sufficiently intelligent and wary not to fall easily into traps of formal fallacies. Where instances of invalidity do arise, this does not necessarily mean that the reasoning itself is spurious. It may well be that the choice of language has been careless so that by means of removing ambiguities or vaguenesses of expression by appropriate interpretation, validity can be restored.

Insolidity arises where the derivation base of an argument is logically inconsistent, that is, dyslogous. In this case, any conclusion is formally valid (the only condition of formal validity is the exclusion of a false conclusion following from a true premiss or from true premisses). Hence, in the case of a dyslogous derivation base, an invalid conclusion is impossible from the outset, and the requirement of formal validity of the conclusion is satisfied, irrespective of what this conclusion may be. Just as invalidity is an unusual phenomenon in judicial reasoning (always provided that all suppressed premisses are taken into account), so insolidity also appears only rarely. Conflicting decisions or principles are, of course, a regular feature in the legal world, but it is an important task of judicial reasoning (resorting to various expedients of legal method) to reconcile or remove the inconsistency that has been identified. Judges dismiss one or more premisses that conflict (thus removing the inconsistency) or they reconcile an apparent conflict by an appropriate interpretation (thus again removing the inconsistency).

R. *v*. Phillips
(1953) 1 All E.R. 617
Legal Area: Torts

***The Facts of the Case:***

The defendant backed his taxi into a small boy on a tricycle. The boy was slightly injured. The boy's mother, from a window in her home seventy yards away saw the tricycle under the cab, but could not see her son. She suffered from nervous shock. The trial judge held that the defendant was under no liability to the mother. The plaintiff appealed.

*The Text of the Argument:*

Denning, L.J.: Every driver can and should foresee that, if he drives negligently, he may injure somebody in the vicinity in some way or other; and he must be responsible for all the injuries which he does in fact cause by his negligence to anyone in the vicinity, whether they are wounds or shocks, unless they are too remote in law to be recovered. If he does by his negligence in fact cause injury by shock, then he should be liable for it unless he is exempted on the grounds of remoteness. ... There was duty of care owed by the taxi driver not only to the boy, but also to his mother. ... Nevertheless, ... the shock in this case is too remote to be a head of damage. ... The taxi cab driver cannot reasonably be expected to have foreseen that his backing would terrify a mother seventy yards away.

*The Logical Structure of the Argument:*

For every $r$ (i.e. driver) and every $s$ (i.e. some person), if $r$ negligently causes $s$ injury by shock then if it is not that $r$ is exempted on the ground of remoteness then $r$ is liable to $s$. The taxi driver negligently causes the mother injury by shock. He is exempted on the ground of remoteness. Therefore, it is not that the taxi driver is liable to the mother.

*Glossary:*

$S$ : ... negligently causes ... injury by shock

$R$ : ... is exempted on the ground of remoteness

$L$ : ... is liable to ...

$a$ : the taxi driver

$o$ : the mother

*Consolidated Solidity and Validity Proof:*

1. $\bigwedge_{r}\bigwedge_{s} C\ Srs\ C\ \bar{R}r\ Lrs$

| | | |
|---|---|---|
| 2. | $Sao$ | |
| 3. | $Ra$ | $/\therefore\ \bar{L}ao$ |
| 4. | $C\ Sao\ C\ \bar{R}a\ Lao$ | 1, U.T. |
| 5. | $A\ \bar{S}ao\ A\ Ra\ Lao$ | 4, S.Dual., D.N. |
| 6. | $A\ Ra\ Lao$ | 5,2, A.E. |

Solid: F-CF unattainable

| | | |
|---|---|---|
| 7. | $Lao$ | CFC |

Invalid: F-CF unattainable

What has gone wrong here? The judgment appears to be straightforward and the reasoning seems impeccable, yet it proves that the conclusion of the argument is invalid. The fault proves to lie in the formalization of the first premiss . The actual words used were to the effect: "If the driver by his negligence in fact causes injury by shock then he is liable for it unless he is exempted on the grounds of remoteness". In the Logical Structure of the Argument, this was rendered as "... if *r* negligently causes *s* injury by shock then if it is not that *r* is exempted on the ground of remoteness then *r* is liable to *s*". At first sight , this appears to be a proper rephrasing, but the problem lies in treating "unless" as "if it is not that". The conclusion of the above argument can be shown to be valid if "unless" is treated here as "if and only if it is not that". In this case the first premiss of the argument would be $\bigwedge\bigwedge_{rs} C\ Srs\ E\ \bar{R}r\ Lrs$ . Probably, this was what the judge meant.

Ethiopia *v*. South Africa
Liberia *v*. South Africa
First Phase. Preliminary Objections
(1962) I.C.J.R. 319
Legal Area: International Law

*The Facts of the Case:*

The relevant part of Article 7 of the South Africa Mandate is: "The Mandatory agrees that, if any dispute whatever should arise between the Mandatory and another Member of the League of Nations relating to the interpretation or application of the provisions of the mandate, such dispute, if it cannot be settled by negotiation, shall be submitted to the Permanent Court of International Justice." One of the questions before the Court was whether there was a dispute between the litigants. In their Dissenting Judgment (pp. 551-552), Judges Spender and Fitzmaurice examine the effect of the words "if it cannot be settled by negotiation".

*The Text of the Argument* (of Judges Spender and Fitzmaurice):

For a dispute to fall within Article 7, it must be a dispute that cannot be settled by negotiation. If it is a dispute that cannot be settled by negotiation then it must be a dispute of a kind that is inherently capable of settlement by negotiation. A dispute concerning the general conduct of a mandate is inherently incapable of settlement by negotiation. Therefore, a dispute concerning the general conduct of a mandate does not fall within Article 7.

*The Logical Structure of the Argument:*

For every *s* (i.e. dispute): if *s* falls within Article 7 then *s* can be settled by negotiation. For every *s*: if it is not that *s* can be settled by negotiation then *s* is inherently capable of settlement by negotiation. For every *s*: if *s* concerns the general conduct of a mandate then it is not that *s* is inherently capable of settlement by negotiation. Therefore, for every *s*: if *s* concerns a general conduct of a mandate then it is not that *s* falls within Article 7.

*Glossary:*

*F* : ... falls within Article 7

*C* : ... can be settled by negotiation

*I* : ... is inherently capable of settlement by negotiation

*G* : ... concerns the general conduct of a mandate

As presented, the argument proves to be valid; however, it raises a particular problem in connection with the interpretation given by Judges Spender and Fitzmaurice to "cannot be settled by negotiation". It appears that they take this expression to mean a dispute which is potentially capable of being settled by negotiation, but which the parties have failed to settle so. The curiosity of the argument is highlighted in the glossary where *C* and *I* appear to carry the same meaning. It may be argued that the wording of Article 7 imports a broader meaning of "cannot" so that it would refer to a dispute which is inherently incapable of settlement or which, if potentially capable of settlement, the parties have failed to settle. If this broader meaning of "cannot" is to be accepted then the second premiss should read:

> If it is not that *s* can be settled by negotiation then it is not that *s* is inherently capable of settlement by negotiation or if *s* is inherently capable of settlement by negotiation then it is not that *s* has been settled by the parties.

Adding to the glossary:

*T* : ... has been settled by the parties

there will be a new argument whose conclusion will prove to be invalid.

*Consolidated Solidity and Validity Proof:*

| | | |
|---|---|---|
| 1. | $\wedge\mathsf{C}\;F\;C$ | |
| 2. | $\wedge\mathsf{C}\;\bar{C}\;\mathsf{A}\;\bar{I}\;\mathsf{C}\;I\;\bar{T}$ | |
| 3. | $\wedge\mathsf{C}\;G\;\bar{I}$ | /.'. $\underline{\wedge\mathsf{C}\;G\;\bar{F}}$ |
| 4. | $\mathsf{C}\;Fi\;Ci$ | 1, U.T. |
| 5. | $\mathsf{A}\;\overline{Fi}\;Ci$ | 4, S.Dual. |
| 6. | $\mathsf{C}\;\overline{Ci}\;\mathsf{A}\;\overline{Ii}\;\mathsf{C}\;Ii\;\overline{Ti}$ | 2, U.T. |
| 7. | $\mathsf{A}\;Ci\;\mathsf{A}\;\overline{Ii}\;\mathsf{A}\;\overline{Ii}\;\overline{Ti}$ | 6, S.Dual., D.N. |
| 8. | $\mathsf{C}\;Gi\;\overline{Ii}$ | 3, U.T. |
| 9. | $\mathsf{A}\;\overline{Gi}\;\overline{Ii}$ | 8, S.Dual. |
| 10. | $\mathsf{A}\;Ci\;\mathsf{A}\;\overline{Ii}\;\overline{Ti}$ | 7, R.P.R., Aut. |

Solid: F-CF unattainable

| | | |
|---|---|---|
| 3a. | $\overline{\wedge}\mathsf{C}\;G\;\bar{F}$ | CFC |

| | | |
|---|---|---|
| 3b. | $v\bar{C}$ *G* $\bar{F}$ | 3a, U.N. |
| 3c. | $\bar{C}$ *Gi* $\bar{F}i$ | 3b, P.T. |
| 3d. | K *Gi Fi* | 3c, CS.Dual., D.N. |
| 3e. | *Gi* , *Fi* | 3d, C.E. |
| 11. | *Ci* | 5,3e, A.E. |
| 12. | $\bar{I}i$ | 9,3e, A.E. |

Invalid: F-CF unattainable

The numeration in the validity proof starts with 3a, in order to make P.T. possible in respect of *i*. There are cases in which it is more expedient to conduct the two proofs separately.

P. & O. Steam Navigation Co. *v*. Shand
(1865) 3 Moor (N.S.) 272
Legal Area: Conflict of Laws

*The Facts of the Case:*

The respondent travelled with the appellant company's ship to Mauritius. On arrival some of his baggage was missing. His ticket included a condition to the effect that the company was not to be liable for damage or loss of baggage. The Mauritius Court held that the law of Mauritius governed the contract and by that law the appellant company was liable despite the exempting clause.

*The Text of the Argument:*

Turner, L.J. (on appeal in Privy Council): ... the Court below held that the law by which the case was to be tried was the French law, which prevails generally in Mauritius, and by that law the appellants were liable. In the argument before their Lordships the latter proposition was not seriously disputed, but it was contended that the Court below should have tried the case by the rules of English law, and that according to these rules the appellants were protected, under the circumstances of the case, by the terms of their contract with the respondent. On his part, however, it was argued that even if the Court below were wrong as to the rule it had governed itself by, yet the judgment was right, even upon the principles of English law.

*The Logical Structure of the Premisses Involved in the Argument:*

French law applies and the appellant company is liable. English law applies and it is not that the appellant company is liable. English law applies and the appellant company is liable.

*Glossary:*

*r* : French law applies
*n* : English law applies
*a* : The appellant company is liable

*Insolidity Proof:*

1. K r a
2. K n $\bar{a}$
3. K n a /∴ ...
4. a 1, C.E.
5. $\bar{a}$ 2, C.E.

Insolid: 4,5: F-CF

or

6. a 3, C.E.

Insolid: 5,6: F-CF

It proves that Premisses 1 and 2 as well as 2 and 3 are inconsistent with each other.

If the Court were framing its own argument rather than merely recounting the conflicting propositions of the parties, it might argue thus: If French law applies then the appellant company is liable. If English law applies then it is not that the appellant company is liable. English law applies. Therefore, it is not that the appellant company is liable. The conclusion of this argument can be proved to be solid as well as valid.

Supposing that the Court were concerned only with the propositions "If English law applies then the appellant company is liable" and "If English law applies then it is not that the appellant company is liable", would these propositions represent inconsistent premisses of an argument? On the surface, it would appear that this is the case, but the following proof shows that it is not so:

*Solidity Proof:*

| | | |
|---|---|---|
| 1. | $\mathsf{C}\,n\,a$ | |
| 2. | $\mathsf{C}\,n\,\bar{a}$ | /∴ ... |
| 3. | $\mathsf{A}\,\bar{n}\,a$ | 1, S.Dual. |
| 4. | $\mathsf{A}\,\bar{n}\,\bar{a}$ | 2, S.Dual. |
| 5. | $\bar{n}$ | 3,4, A.A.C. |

Solid: F–CF unattainable

Something appears to be unusual here, for intuitively the premisses of the argument are inconsistent, yet proved to be consistent. The explanation is that "inconsistency" has a different meaning in ordinary language from its technical use in logic. Technically, two (or more) propositions are inconsistent if and only if their conjunction is a dyslogy. If two propositions are such that they cannot both be true but they can both be false (contraries) or they cannot both be false but can both be true (subcontraries), they are not *logically* inconsistent.

Insolidity may be entrenched within the very core of a legal system. This can be seen when the following two fundamental principles of constitutional law are examined:

(1) Parliament can make or unmake any law whatsoever.

(2) Parliament cannot bind its successor.

The Paradox of Parliamentary Sovereignty, whereby on the one hand it is postulated that no law is beyond Parliamentary competence, while on the other hand it is claimed that one kind of law is beyond such competence, can be unravelled by symbolizing the two propositions and by subjecting their conjunction to a dyslogy test.

*The Logical Structure of the Principles:*

For every *w* (i.e. law): Parliament can make *w* and Parliament can unmake *w*. It is not that Parliament can make the law which binds its successor.

*Glossary:*

*M* : ... can make ...

*U* : ... can unmake ...

*a* : Parliament

*i* : the law which binds the successor of Parliament

*Dyslogy Test:*

| | | |
|---|---|---|
| 1. | $K \bigwedge_{w} K\ Maw\ Uaw\ \bar{M}ai$ | |
| 2. | $\bigwedge_{w} K\ Maw\ Uaw$ | 1, C.E. |
| 3. | $K\ Mai\ Uai$ | 2, U.T. |
| 4. | $\bar{M}ai$ | 1, C.E. |
| 5. | $Mai$ | 3, C.E. |

Dyslogy: 4,5: F-CF

Since the two principles in question proved to be inconsistent, the logical effect of their being used as premisses of an argument in the field of constitutional law would be the insolidity of any conclusion derived from them. Since insolidity produces not sterility but overfertility of conclusions (for any conclusion whatsoever follows from a dyslogous derivation base), one could validly (but not necessarily soundly) argue:

Parliament can make or unmake any law
Parliament cannot bind its successor
__________
The parliamentary system is futile

## III. Services of Logic in Dealing with Some Special Legal Problems

### 1. *Logical Testing of the Validity of Gifts*

The counter-formula method can render useful services to lawyers when it comes to the handling of problems posed by the limitation of estates in real property. In this area of their work, legal expertise acquired by experience and the following of patterns of decided cases which have acquired authoritative status may suffice for most practical purposes. However, in this way irrefutable proofs of logical validity of the claimed conclusions can never be provided. Moreover, once the requisite logical technique is mastered, it proves that the logical approach to the solution of the problems involved is efficient and expedient.

Consider the following problem: There is a gift of property on trust for the grandchildren of A. In which of the following situations is the gift valid?

(a) A is alive and there is at least one grandchild of his alive?

(b) A is dead, but there is at least one grandchild of his alive?

(c) A is alive, but no grandchild of his is alive.

(d) A is dead and no grandchild of his is alive.

The relevant propositions of law are as follows:

(1) If there is a grandchild of A alive at the time of the gift then the gift is valid, the class of beneficiaries closes, and A's grandchildren alive at the time of the gift participate in the gift and no grandchild of A born after the time of gift participates.

(2) If there is no grandchild of A alive at the time of the gift then if and only if the property must vest within the perpetuity period then the gift is valid and if the gift is valid then all A's grandchildren participate

in the gift; if it is invalid then none of A's grandchildren participate in the gift.

(3) If and only if all A's grandchildren are ascertained within 21 years of relevant lives-in-being then the property must vest within the perpetuity period.

(4) If a grandchild of A may be born more then 21 years after relevant lives-in-being then it is not the case that all A's grandchildren are ascertained within 21 years of relevant lives-in-being.

(5) If and only if A is dead at the time of the gift then A's children are relevant lives-in-being.

(6) If all A's children are relevant lives-in-being then A's grandchildren are ascertained within 21 years of relevant lives-in-being.

(7) If A is alive at the time of the gift then A may beget another child and a grandchild of A may be born more than 21 years after relevant lives-in-being.

This is a four-part problem. Each part is an argument in which the premisses are the seven relevant propositions of law and the propositions about the fact-situations described under (a), (b), (c), and (d). If the claimed conclusion of an argument proves to be valid then the gift is valid; if it proves to be invalid then the gift is invalid.

*Glossary:*

*a* : All A's grandchildren participate in the gift

*e* : None of A's grandchildren participate in the gift

*i* : All A's grandchildren alive at the time of the gift participate in it

*o* : No grandchild of A born after the time of the gift participates in it

*m* : There is at least one grandchild of A alive at the time of the gift

*g* : The gift is valid

*s* : The class of beneficiaries closes

*p* : The property must vest within the perpetuity period

*w* : All A's grandchildren are ascertained within 21 years of relevant lives-in-being

*n* : A grandchild of A may be born more than 21 years after relevant lives-in-being *v :* A is alive at the time of the gift

*r :* All A's children are relevant lives-in-being

*c :* A may beget another child not a relevant life-in-being

*Validity Tests:*

1. $C m K K K g s i o$
2. $C \bar{m} K K E p g C g a C \bar{g} e$
3. $E w p$
4. $C n \bar{w}$
5. $E \bar{v} r$
6. $C r w$
7. $C v K c n$

8a. $K v m$

8b. $K \bar{v} m$

8c. $K v \bar{m}$

8d. $K \bar{v} \bar{m}$ $\quad\therefore\quad \underline{g}$

Note that Premiss 8 varies according to the fact-situation involved.

For all four arguments the decision-procedure is as follows:

| | | |
|---|---|---|
| 9. | $\bar{g}$ | CFC |
| 10. | $A \bar{m} K K K g s i o$ | 1, S.Dual. |
| 11. | $A m K K E p g A \bar{g} a A g e$ | 2, S.Dual., D.N. |
| 12. | $A m K K K A \bar{p} g A p \bar{g}$ - $A \bar{g} a A g e$ | 11, B.Diss. |
| 13. | $A \bar{w} p$ | 3, B.Diss., C.E. |
| 14. | $A w \bar{p}$ | 3, B.Diss., C.E. |
| 15. | $A \bar{n} \bar{w}$ | 4, S.Dual. |
| 16. | $A v r$ | 5, B.Diss., C.E., D.N. |
| 17. | $A \bar{v} \bar{r}$ | 5, B.Diss., C.E. |
| 18. | $A \bar{r} w$ | 6, S.Dual. |
| 19. | $A \bar{v} K c n$ | 7, S.Dual. |

The four derivations now continue separately:

| | | | |
|---|---|---|---|
| (a) | 20. | m | 8a, C.E. |
| | 21. | $\bar{m}$ | 9,10, C.A.E. |
| | Valid: | 20,21: F-CF | |
| (b) | 20. | m | 8b, C.E. |
| | 21. | K K K g s i o | 10,20, A.E. |
| | 22. | g | 21, C.E. |
| | Valid: | 9,22: F-CF | |
| (c) | 20. | v | 8c, C.E. |
| | 21. | $\bar{m}$ | 8c, C.E. |
| | 22. | K K K A $\bar{p}$ g A p $\bar{g}$ - A $\bar{g}$ a A g e | 12,21, A.E. |
| | 23. | A $\bar{p}$ g | 22, C.E. |
| | 24. | A g e | 22, C.E. |
| | 25. | $\bar{p}$ | 9,23, A.E. |
| | 26. | e | 9,24, A.E. |
| | 27. | $\bar{w}$ | 13,25, A.E. |
| | 28. | $\bar{r}$ | 18,27, A.E. |
| | 29. | K c n | 19,20, A.E. |
| | 30. | c | 29, C.E. |
| | 31. | n | 29, C.E. |
| | Invalid: | F-CF unattainable | |
| (d) | 20. | $\bar{v}$ | 8d, C.E. |
| | 21. | $\bar{m}$ | 8d, C.E. |
| | 22. | K K K A $\bar{p}$ g A p $\bar{g}$ - A $\bar{g}$ a A g e | 12,21, A.E. |
| | 23. | A $\bar{p}$ g | 22, C.E. |
| | 24. | A g e | 22, C.E. |

| | | |
|---|---|---|
| 25. | $r$ | 16,20, A.E. |
| 26. | $w$ | 18,25, A.E. |
| 27. | $\bar{p}$ | 9,23, A.E. |
| 28. | $p$ | 13,26, A.E. |

Valid: 27,28: F-CF

Thus the result of the above logical testing is that the gift is invalid only if at the time of the gift A is alive, but no grandchild of his is alive. In the other situations, the gift is valid.

### *2. The Logical Aspect of Ambiguities in Law*

A legal expression is ambiguous for the purposes of law if it has more than one legally relevant meaning. An ambiguity is semantic if it is due to a variety of meanings which words, phrases, or sentences have acquired in linguistic usage. As to words, examples of such ambiguities are "right" (which in its wide sense relates to a situation where someone is permitted to do something and possibly also obligated to do this and which in its narrow sense relates to a situation where someone is permitted but not obligated to do something) and "possession" (which has different meanings in the law of property and in criminal law).

The sentence "Commerce and traffic between the member States shall be absolutely free" serves as an example of a rather complex semantic ambiguity. The ambiguity results here from multiple meanings which the words "free" and "absolutely" as well as the phrase "commerce and traffic" convey. Semantic ambiguities are a source of absurd conclusions in inferences if they are not attended by assignment of different symbolic expressions to each meaning.

An ambiguity is syntactic if it is due to the construction of sentence. Such ambiguities ("amphibolies") occur less frequently in highly inflected languages or in those which have genders for their nouns. These linguistic features provide devices for identifying precise interrelations between parts of a sentence. Since English does not have such features, syntactic ambiguities are of frequent occurrence in it. A simple example of a syntactic ambiguity is the following advertisement:

For Sale: Perfect gentleman's outfit.

This can mean that the present owner of the outfit is described as perfect or that the outfit itself is described as perfect or that the outfit is described to be perfect as a gentleman's outfit.

The logical structure of any ambiguous expression is an adjunction with several adjuncts. The removal of ambiguity involves elimination of those adjuncts which are inapplicable for the given purpose. The relevant rejection has the formal pattern of Adjunction Elimination. The process of reasoning which leads to the rejection of certain meanings in the removal of ambiguity for particular cases goes beyond the scope of legal logic. It is largely a task of legal interpretation.

Whether an ambiguity be semantic or syntactic, it can be exposed by casting the ambiguous expression into a logical form that represents all ambiguous meanings. While in the case of a semantic ambiguity different predicators are required for expressing alternative meanings, in the case of a syntactic ambiguity the alternative meanings are expressed by different combinations of the same predicators with hypotacts or by different placements of predications.

A simple legal illustration of a semantic ambiguity is the following:

All adult inhabitants of the municipality of Easton are entitled to vote in the municipal elections.

The ambiguity arises here from the uncertainty as to whether the word "inhabitant" means only those inhabitants who are also the citizens of the country or whether it means aliens as well. The ambiguity can be expressed in symbols by employing different superscripts for the predicator which refers to the adult inhabitants.

$I^1$ : ... is an adult inhabitant whatever his citizenship

$I^2$ : ... is an adult inhabitant who is a citizen

$V$ : ... is entitled to vote in the municipal elections

The ambiguity can now be expressed by the following formula:

$$A \wedge C\, I^1 V \wedge C\, I^2 V$$

When it is established by appropriate legal techniques which of the two meanings of "inhabitant" is to be rejected, the corresponding adjunct is excluded from the formula by the application of Adjunction Elimination and the other adjunct is posited. The exclusion takes place by negating the adjunct representing the rejected meaning. In the case where the first adjunct is excluded, the procedure is as follows:

1. $A \wedge C\, I^1 V \wedge C\, I^2 V$
2. $\bar{\wedge} C\, I^1 V$ /.'. $\underline{\wedge C\, I^2 V}$
3. $\wedge C\, I^2 V$ 1,2, A.E.

A relatively simple legal illustration of a syntactic ambiguity is the following:

> Such violations shall include plunder of property, wanton destruction of cities or devastation not justified by military necessity.

The ambiguity lies here in the uncertainty as to whether the phrase "not justified by military necessity" qualifies all the expressions referring to the prohibited actions or only the expression "devastation".

The ambiguity can be exposed by employing brackets as follows:

> Such violations shall include [(plunder of property), (wanton destruction of cities) or (devastation)] (not justified by military necessity).

> Such violations shall include (plunder of property), (wanton destruction of cities) or (devastation not justified by military necessity).

*Glossary:*

*V* : ... is a violation

*P* : ... is a plunder of property

*W* : ... is wanton destruction of cities

*D* : ... is devastation

*J* : ... is justified by military necessity

The ambiguity that appears here can be expressed by means of a predicational adjunction in which the adjunctor is written on the first line and the two adjuncts are written separately on the second and the third lines.

$$\mathrm{A}\,-$$
$$\wedge\mathrm{C\,K\,A\,A}\,PWD\bar{J}V\,-$$
$$\wedge\mathrm{C\,A\,A}\,PW\,\mathrm{K}\,D\bar{J}V$$

When the formula as arranged above is inspected, it appears that the two adjuncts are both subjunctions which have different antecedents but identical consequents. After it has been decided which adjunct must be excluded, the remaining adjunct can be posited by applying Adjunction Elimination.

### 3. *The Logical Aspect of Inconsistencies and Gaps in Law*

An antinomy is present in law where two legal norms are antagonistic to each other. This antagonism can be such that the observance of one norm makes the observance of another norm materially impossible. Thus if a norm directs that all cattle in a certain area affected by a disease shall be destroyed and burnt and another norm directs that all cattle in the same area shall be subjected to veterinary examination, immunization, and treatment, there is certainly an antinomy. However, such an antinomy is not directly of logical relevance, for the logical inconsistency of the norms in question cannot be displayed by merely showing that they are at odds with each other. An antinomy of logical relevance will appear here if a suppressed assumption is made explicit according to which the first course of action excludes the second one. An antinomy of logical relevance is directly recognizable where the presence of two antagonistic norms produces a dyslogy under the principles governing the normative universe.

The antinomies which occur within the same legal system are of the greatest juristic importance. However, lawyers are sometimes also concerned with those antinomies which arise between norms belonging to different legal systems or between norms of which one belongs to a legal system and another to a system of morals or to some other non-legal normative system. This may happen in contexts of private international law, of conflicts between law and morals, etc. An antinomy is a normative state of affairs which is usually regarded as undesirable. Thus by interpretation and other means of normative construction, lawyers try to remove antinomies. All civilized legal systems contain principles whose function is to resolve antinomies occurring within them, notably *lex superior derogat legi inferiori*, *lex posterior derogat legi priori*, and *lex specialis derogat legi generali*. The resolution of antinomies is a phase in the legal process; in its initial stage, antinomies do exist and their identification is an indispensable preliminary for their removal. It depends on the given legal or other normative system whether or not all antinomies can be resolved. Irremovable antinomies are conceivable and occur in actual fact in some normative systems.

Logically, an irremovable antinomy in a legal system is an instance of genuine contradiction of norms, from which - if it is present in a normative derivation base - any conclusion can be validly (but not solidly) drawn by virtue of the *Ex Falso Quodlibet* theorem. The logical effect of an irremovable antinomy is not destruction of either contradictory norm or of both norms. Such an effect can only be achieved by the operation of a special principle, which may or may not be available for dealing with a given instance of antinomy. A legal system which admits of irremovable antinomies is surely a defective normative system; however, by this token alone it need not be an unworkable system. For its residual soundness may lend it viability, usefulness, and even decency for regulating human conduct.

In order to identify an inconsistency in law, it is necessary to put norms into an appropriate logical form and then to demonstrate that they produce dyslogy. In the present book, the norms are conceived as indicatives. This manner of their logical treatment does not affect their directive force nor does it exclude a different logical construction of norms, for example, a construction based on a system of the logic of imperatives.

Elementary forms of legal norms can be constructed as dyadic predications. The characteristically normative element is represented by a relator, which stands for a concept rendered by ordinary language mostly by a deontic verb (e.g. "ought-to", "may"). As a dyadic predication, a legal norm constitutes a relation whose fore-term stands for the norm-subject (i.e. the entity to which the norm is addressed), the after-term for the norm-object (i.e. the conduct regulated by the norm), and the relator for the norm-nexus (i.e. the link between the two other elements). By symbolizing the norm-subject as "$s$", the norm-object as "$c$", and the norm-nexus as "$N$", the formula for the legal norm in general is $Nsc$, where both terms are synopic hypotacts with limited range of application. This limitation imports that their application instances can occur only within the range of the addressees of legal norms and of the conduct regulated by legal norms respectively. $Nsc$ is an open formula; to render it a closed formula (i.e. one which would represent a complete indicative thought-formation), it is necessary to quantify its (synopic) hypotacts.

There are several varieties of norm-nexus resulting from the basic meanings of deontic verbs combined with the *performative factors* "to be carried out" and "to be refrained from". For the purpose of the present system, the following deontic verbs are required: "ought-to", "may", and "can". In the actual legal language of law, the deontic verbs "must" and "shall" are frequently used in the sense which coincides with that of "ought-to" used here to generally convey the idea of obligation. The linguistic difference between "must" and "shall" is irrelevant for logical analyses, since it is mainly one of emphasis or of conative force which the corresponding sentences are intended to carry.

The combination of the three deontic verbs used here with the two performative factors yields the following six varieties of norm-nexus and their corresponding symbolic expressions:

| | |
|---|---|
| ought to carry out: | $O^a$ |
| ought to refrain from: | $O^e$ |
| may carry out: | $M^a$ |
| may refrain from: | $M^e$ |
| can carry out: | $C^a$ |
| can refrain from: | $C^e$ |

Note that "can" is used here in a normative sense and not in the sense of physical or mental ability; it is roughly equivalent to "is entitled to".

The meanings of the six varieties of norm-nexus are the following:

$O^a$ conveys a positive duty (i.e. the duty to do something),

$O^e$ conveys a negative duty (i.e. the duty not to do something),

$M^a$ conveys a positive right in the narrow sense (i.e. the right to do something without a duty to do so),

$M^e$ conveys a negative right in the narrow sense (i.e. the right to not to do something without a duty to do so),

$C^a$ conveys a positive right in the wide sense (i.e. the right to do something with or without a duty to do so),

$C^e$ conveys a negative right in the wide sense (i.e. the right not to do something with or without a duty to do so).

Either term in a norm-relation can be either synopic or stigmic. In the former case, its completed logical form requires quantification either by the universalizer or by the particularizer. Accordingly, there are the following principal kinds of norm:

(1) General-abstract norms, in which both terms are synopic (e.g. $\bigwedge_{s}\bigvee_{c} O^{a} sc$);

(2) General-concrete norms, in which the fore-term is synopic and the after-term is stigmic (e.g. $\bigwedge_{s} M^{e} so$);

(3) Singular-abstract norms, in which the fore-term is stigmic and the after-term is synopic (e.g. $\bigwedge_{c} C^{a} uc$);

(4) Singular-concrete norms, in which both terms are stigmic (e.g. $O^{e} uo$).

The following principal relationships hold between two logical expressions of singular-concrete norms:

$\mathrm{C}\, O^{a}uo\, C^{a}uo$ , $\mathrm{C}\, O^{e}uo\, C^{e}uo$ , $\bar{\mathrm{K}}\, O^{a}uo\, O^{e}uo$ , $\bar{\mathrm{K}}\, O^{a}uo\, M^{a}uo$ , $\bar{\mathrm{K}}\, O^{e}uo\, M^{e}uo$ , $\mathrm{C}\, M^{a}uo\, C^{a}uo$ , $\mathrm{C}\, M^{e}uo\, C^{e}uo$ , $\mathrm{E}\, M^{a}uo\, M^{e}uo$ , $\mathrm{A}\, C^{a}uo\, C^{e}uo$ .

These relationships hold both for normatively closed and for normatively open legal systems, the former being such in which gaps are excluded and the latter being such in which gaps can occur. In the normatively closed systems, the following further relationships hold:

$\bar{\mathrm{E}}\, O^{a}uo\, C^{e}uo$ and $\bar{\mathrm{E}}\, O^{e}uo\, C^{a}uo$ .

In the normatively open systems, the following further relationships hold instead:

$\bar{\mathrm{K}}\, O^{a}uo\, C^{e}uo$ and $\bar{\mathrm{K}}\, O^{e}uo\, C^{a}uo$ .

All above relationships hold also between two general-abstract norms, between two general-concrete norms, and between two singular-abstract norms, provided that in each case their derivates are the singular-concrete norms which correspond to the above formal patterns.

The coterminous norm-relations are liable to represent inconsistent norms if their logical expressions are constituted by the relators $O^{a}$ and $O^{e}$, $O^{a}$ and $M^{a}$ , $O^{a}$ and $M^{e}$, $O^{e}$ and $M^{e}$, $O^{e}$ and $M^{a}$ , $O^{a}$ and $C^{e}$, and $O^{e}$ and $C^{a}$. There can be inconsistencies also between the norms whose logical expressions are such that one belongs to the range of application of the other. In this case, they are present if they can produce inconsistencies according to the above stated principles. Thus $\bigwedge_{s}\bigwedge_{c} O^{a}{}_{sc}$ and $O^{e}{}_{uo}$ represent inconsistent norms, because the application of Universal Stigmication to the first formula yields $O^{a}{}_{uo}$, whose conjunction with the second formula produces a dyslogy under the relevant deontic principle.

A gap is present in law where there is no legal provision *required by the law itself* and the relevant legal system does not contain a universal principle which would supply a norm for otherwise unprovided cases. A legal system which contains the *closure principle* (also called "the hermetic principle" or "the residual negative principle"), according to which *Whatever is not legally prohibited is legally permitted*, excludes all gaps in it and is in this sense normatively closed. The existence of the closure principle is, however, a purely contingent matter; in no way is it a presupposition of all legal systems. It can be formulated as follows:

$$\bigwedge_{s}\bigwedge_{c} K\, \bar{\bar{E}}\, O^{a}{}_{sc}\, C^{e}{}_{sc}\, \bar{\bar{E}}\, O^{e}{}_{sc}\, C^{a}{}_{sc}$$

The following situations illustrate the existence of gaps in law:

> A treaty provides: "The boundary between the territories of the High Contracting Parties in the Eastern Alps is the line established by the local custom". There is no pertinent local custom nor is there any norm under which it would be obligatory for the Parties or any other legal authority of the relevant legal system to provide the requisite missing norm.
>
> A statute provides: "The employers of this industry shall pay the wages to their skilled workers which are no less than those specified in the Fourth Schedule appended to the present statute." There is no Fourth Schedule nor is there any norm under which it would be obligatory for the competent law-making authority to supply the requisite missing norm.

The logical aspect of the above two legal situations can be expressed as a conjunction whose one conjunct represents the affirmation of the existence of a norm and whose other conjunct represents the negation of the existence of this norm. Symbolizing the existence of the norm in question by " $e$ ", the relevant formula is $K e \bar{e}$, which is obviously a dyslogy. From it as a premiss, any conclusion whatsoever follows under the *Ex Falso Quodlibet* theorem.

### 4. *Logical Conceivability of* Non-liquet *Declarations*

Particularly international lawyers have addressed themselves to the problem as to whether a court is legally entitled to declare that it is unable to make a decision in a case because of the absence of law required for the decision. The technical term of this refraining from the decision sought by the parties to a legal dispute is "*non liquet*". Whether or not *non liquet* is an entity or non-entity in the international (or any other) legal system depends above all on whether or not it is logically conceivable. A preliminary for answering this question is exploration of the deontic structure of law.

The deontic structure of law consists of the relationships of legally relevant states of affairs involving the same norm-subject or the same norm-subject range and the same norm-object or the same norm-object range but differing in respect of their specific quality. This quality is expressed by adjectives such as "obligatory", "forbidden", and "permitted" and by substantives such as "obligation", "prohibition", and "permission". These and other words widely used to convey the relevant ideas (e.g. "duty" and "right") are ambiguous even in technical legal language. In order to deal with their ambiguities and to achieve a terminology adequate for a fundamental analysis of the present problem , the above words have to be either abandoned altogether and replaced with semantically uncommitted words, or they have to be redefined and somewhat modified where feasible.

The first alternative would yield, of course, the most appropriate linguistic vehicles for purely theoretical purposes, however, it would have the disadvantage of a low communicative value for professional lawyers who (in contrast to pharmacists or physicians) are reluctant to spend their time on learning a new technical language which would appear rather fancy to them. Therefore, the second alternative is chosen for the present purposes, although it, too, is not fully satisfactory, because it involves hazards of misleading connotations of the root-words employed - connotations hanging over from their normal ambiguous use even where a new shape has been given to them by an unusual use of a suffix. However, this drawback seems to be of relatively minor consequence for alert legal scholars.

Before the attempt can be made to construct a theoretically satisfactory deontic system of law, the following matters have to be settled:

(1) "Deontic" in the present context relates to all forms of normative ideas, consequently, to duties rights, permissions, etc., regardless whether these are present or absent. Hence it relates also to the negation of normative ideas.

(2) The deontic words employed here are meant in an ethically neutral sense. That is, moral goodness or badness is "bracketed out" in their use.

(3) The negation of a norm or a normative state of affairs does not necessarily mean that it yields another norm or a normative state of affairs. What this negation yields may thus not be a legal entity but certain non-legal entity which is still significant for legal reasoning.

Norms can be expressed in standard forms by employing deontic verbs (as set out in the previous section). The deontic verbs are so fixed in English that it is impossible to modify them without excessive linguistic strain in order to obtain semi-neologisms needed for an adequate exposition of the deontic structure of law. Therefore, in the subsequent exposition, adjectives are employed instead. Accordingly, a standard form of norm can be rendered as follows:

Carrying out of $c$ is obligatory for $s$

The corresponding norm with the negative performative factor is:

Refraining from *c* is obligatory for *s*

The main task of deontic logic consists in the determination of logical relations between those concepts which are signified by deontic verbs or by deontic adjectives. For dealing with these relations, the norm-subject or the norm-subject range and the norm-object or the norm-object range are regarded as constant in every instance of operation with deontic concepts. Thus for the purpose of establishing a basic framework of deontic logic, their expression can be dispensed with. It is possible also to eliminate the expression of the concept of performatory factor by admitting an additional deontic adjective as a deontic primitive. The following exposition employs a single performatory factor and, correspondingly, two deontic primitives in the guise of deontic adjectives.

The expression of a simple deontic state of affairs has two components: (1) a deontic functor (e.g. "is obligatory"), (2) a deontic hypotact (usually but ambiguously called "deontic argument"), which may be called "*incidence*". The concept "incidence" denotes the instance of conduct of the given norm-subject in any given normatively significant circumstance. If the symbol "$O$" is assigned to "is obligatory" and the symbol "$i$" to "incidence", $Oi$ can be conceived as a monadic predication representing a deontic state of affairs or a deontic modality (framed as a predication). It can be treated according to the principles and methods of predicational calculus. Since only one deontic hypotact is employed throughout the present system, it is not necessary to express it. Thus the formula stated above could be rendered by a single italicized capital letter (in keeping with the abbreviated predicational notation).

A list, subsequently to be expanded, of deontic functors can now be provided:

Obligatory ( $O$ ) - referring to a duty to carry out something.

Prohibitory ( *H* ) - referring to a duty to refrain from something.

Permissory ( *P* ) - referring to a general right to carry out something whether or not there is a duty to carry it out.

Dispensory ( *D* ) - referring to a general right to refrain from something whether or not there is a duty to refrain from it.

Licensory ( *L* ) - referring to a right to carry out something without there being a duty to carry it out.

Concessory ( *C* ) - referring to a right to refrain from something without there being a duty to refrain from it.

The artificiality of the words "permissory" ("permitted" sounds more natural!), "dispensory", "licensory", and "concessory" may produce some linguistic discomfort. However, these words have the advantage of fitting well into normal English and of providing the requisite technical terms at the same time (intimating by their very unusuality that they are intended to convey specific meanings).

It is possible to construct a deontic system which contains the postulate according to which $\bar{E}\,O\,D$ and $\bar{E}\,H\,P$ (where the capital italics stand for deontic modalities expressed in the abbreviated predicational notation). This postulate imports two versions of the closure principle of legal systems. It is also possible to postulate $\bar{K}\,O\,D$ and $\bar{K}\,H\,P$ . The first postulate set relates to those legal systems which are normatively closed; the second postulate set relates to those legal systems which are normatively open.

For the exposition of the structure of normatively open deontic systems the following additional deontic functors are required:

Extratensory ( *T* ) - referring to the absence of any relevant duty and right.

Prepensory ( *E* ) - referring to what is extratensory or dispensory.

Premissory ( *I* ) - referring to what is extratensory or permissory.

The following formulae represent characteristic features of normatively open deontic systems:

ETKEI, EOĒ, EHĪ, CTE, CTI, CDE, CPI
The total universe of the normatively open deontic systems is expressed by AEI.

By reference to the above analysis and discussion, an attempt can now be made to answer the question as to whether, and in what sense, *non liquet* is conceivable in a legal system. It is conceivable, if a legal system can be regarded as being normatively open. A legal system must be regarded as normatively open if it does not contain the closure principle. Unfortunately, the terms "right" and "permission" are often ambiguously used to refer not only to licensory and to permissory deontic states of affairs but also to premissory and to extratensory deontic states of affairs. The lack of requisite conceptual articulation underlying these ambiguities imports loose and vague legal thought liable to trick many legal minds into acceptance of views they may either not hold at all or would hold on material grounds that may be available or discoverable by appropriate intellectual effort.

As to international law, there is no conclusive evidence that it contains the closure principle. Until the existence of this principle in it can be proved, it must be regarded as normatively open; accordingly, *non liquet* declarations by international courts are not excluded. International judges, ostensibly labouring under misconceptions provenant from faulty legal theory have shown great ingenuity in the avoidance of these declarations. Perhaps they will continue to be reluctant to declare *non liquet* even in the future, despite the fact that technological developments have produced international legal problems where not long ago State action or interest was considered never to extend. But they can do so only by surreptitiously engaging in law-creative activity.

## Retrospect and Prospect

In this book I have hazarded not only to swim against strong currents of legal thought adverse to any formal treatment of legal problems, but occasionally I have also ventured to diverge from some beaten tracks of logicians, notably in the area of logical expression. Because legal logic is the application of logic in the field of one of the most important practical activities, the work on it requires attention to certain matters ostensibly overlooked, or underrated in their significance, by those who work on the theoretical foundations of logic or who teach logic to students of philosophy.

Thus the ambiguities in logical terminology may not disturb those whose mind is accustomed to move in the logical universe of discourse. They *do* disturb, however, outsiders to logic, who expect from logic the highest precision in all respects. Further, the currently employed logical notations - which do not represent the ultimate in sign economy and readability or operability of formulae - may be quite adequate for dealing with the foundations of logic or for illustrative didactic purposes. Where, however, very complex formulae have to be handled, which happens when important instances of legal thought require logical treatment, the improvement of notation becomes a task of the first order.

These considerations have led me to try to develop an adequate logical terminology and a satisfactory logical notation for legal logic. By not shunning the creation of artificial terms, a further improvement of logical terminology is feasible, so that every logical term would be free from *any* ambiguity ( even if ordinary language or any other extra-logical technical language is taken into account).

Also the notation employed in this book so far can further be improved, namely by replacing the capital letters used for logical operators with appropriate artificial signs. In this way it is possible to write better articulated and more easily surveyable formulae.

In the foregoing expositions, I have remained rather conservative in terminological and notational innovations, considering that any radical revision in these areas is a task for an international cooperative effort of logicians and not one to be performed by individual writers in books on logic in general or on applications of logic, who would prejudice the communication of their thoughts by too esoteric expressional expedients.

What I have supplied as logical instruments for analyzing legal thought is only a part of that which logic can set at the disposal of lawyers. A great deal more by way of logical equipment is contained in the theories of polyadic relations, of logical types, of definite descriptions, of the quantification of predicators, etc. I have not drawn from the wealth of these theories in order not to frighten the average lawyer away from legal logic altogether, and in order not to write an oversized book. However, for those who have understood this book, it should not be too difficult to derive benefits from any part of logic for their further study or research.

I have also abstained here from dealing with the calculi of extensions, intensions, imperatives, interrogatives, and optatives, which are all of interest to lawyers. These aspects of logic are treated in I. Tammelo & H. Schreiner, *Grundzüge und Grundverfahren der Rechtslogik*, vol.II, 1977 (Verlag Dokumentation, München). Out of the Counter-formula Method, further decision-procedures have been developed by my Salzburg and Sydney colleagues, namely the Contraconjunctive Variant of the Counter-formula Method (Gabriël Moens), the Iso-formula Method (Ivanhoe Tebaldeschi and Gabriël Moens), and the Elimination Method (Helmut Schreiner). So far their expositions have been published in German or in Italian, viz. I. Tammelo & Gabriel Moëns, *Logische Verfahren der juristischen Begründung*, 1976 (Springer-Verlag, Wien & New York); I. Tammelo & I. Tebaldeschi, *Studi di logica giuridica*, 1976 (Dott.A. Giuffrè, Milano); and I. Tammelo & H. Schreiner (eds.), *Strukturierungen und Entscheidungen im Rechtsdenken*, 1978 (Springer-Verlag, Wien & New York).

In the Appendices some possibilities of innovation of logical terminology and notation will be indicated and experimented with and an outline of a system will be provided in which each principal method of legal reasoning has a place.

## APPENDICES

### A. *Innovation of Names and Signs for Logical Operators*

The practical aims of legal logic raise terminological and notational problems, which need attention in order to achieve not only precision and adequacy in both areas but also expediency. Where required, I made choices above among existing alternatives or ventured minor innovations. I hesitated to resort to a more radical approach, which would involve artificial terms and signs. There is scope for this approach if adequacy of utterance to thought with the least expenditure of expressional devices is to be achieved in logic. In this appendix I shall make the corresponding proposals in the region of logical operators.

Even in the technical use of language, neologisms or artificial signs tend to evoke uneasiness; even among experts they are liable to create the impression of being strange, odd, or ugly. Usually, this reaction is only temporary. If the proposed innovations prove to be sound, they are accepted in due course, or they provide stimulus for finding even better solutions for the problems involved.

The notation employed in this book so far can be improved by replacing the capital letters used for the dyadic operators with appropriate artificial signs. This would render the formulae in which they occur better surveyable and would have the advantage of allowing expedient combined signs to be created.

The dyadic operators ( = junctors ) employed in this book are distinguished by prefixes "sub-", "con-", etc. This gives rise to words some of which belong to ordinary language, or to an extra-logical technical language, where they have meanings which are different from those they are intended to have in logic (e.g. "subjunction", "conjunction"). To avoid *any* ambiguity here, the five junctors employed in this book can be distinguished by means of five capital vowels attached as prefixes to the word "junctor" with a hyphen:

| C | A | K | E | D |
|---|---|---|---|---|
| I-junctor | A-junctor | O-junctor | E-junctor | U-junctor |

The corresponding junctions are to be called then "I-junction", "A-junction", etc. A formula governed by a junctor is to be called then "I-junct", "A-junct", etc.

Suitable artificial signs for replacing the capital letters so far used for the junctors are available on the type-element No. 6522909 of the now widely used IBM Selectric typewriter. As to ordinary typewriters, the corresponding signs can be produced by combining strokes with apostrophes or with hyphens. For reading these signs, words can be created by adding "k" to the vowel indicating each junctor. All this will appear from the following:

| | C | A | K | E | D |
|---|---|---|---|---|---|
| IBM Selectric Typewriter: | ⌡ | ⌋ | ⌈ | ∫ | ⌠ |
| Ordinary Typewriter: | ✓ | _/ | /¯ | ✓' | /' |
| Abbreviated Name: | Ik | Ak | Ok | Ek | Uk |

The above proposed terminological innovations would require the following modifications in the names or the abbreviated names of the rules of the counter-formula method:

| | |
|---|---|
| I-Junction Duality | (I.Dual.) |
| U-Junction Duality | (U.Dual.) |
| E-Junction Dissection | (E.Diss.) |
| Contra-I-Junction Duality | (CI.Dual.) |
| Contra-U-Junction Duality | (CU.Dual.) |
| Contra-A-Junction Duality | (CA.Dual.) |
| Contra-O-Junction Duality | (CO.Dual.) |
| Contra-E-Junction Dissection | (CE.Diss.) |
| O-Junction Elimination | (O.E.) |
| O-Junction Contraction | (O.C.) |
| A-Junction Elimination | (A.E.) |

A-Junction Contraction (A.C.)

O-Junctive A-Junction Elimination (O.A.E.)

Autological A-Junction Contraction (A.A.C.)

A negative junctor can be expressed by a combined sign in which a bar is placed on top of a junctor, for example, ⌡̄ , ⌠̄ , ⌈̄ . Where it is necessary to distinguish formulae according to the area of logic to which they belong, this can be done by prepending a dot to an indicative junctor, an exclamation mark to an imperative junctor, a question mark to an interrogative junctor, and an apostrophe to an optative junctor. This would give rise, for example, to the following signs: ·⌡ , !⌈̄ , ?⌠ , '⌡̄ .

### B. *Exercises in the Counter-formula Method*

In the following exercises, the operators will be expressed by the artificial signs introduced in Appendix A. In the justification columns of these exercises, the modified abbreviated names of the relevant rules will be employed.

I. *Consolidated Solidity and Validity Proof:*

Supply the justification column!

1. ⌡ $\bar{p}$ q
2. ⌠ ⌡ $\bar{p}$ q r
3. ⌡ r $\bar{p}$ /∴ q
---
4. ⌡ p q ...
5. ⌡ ⌡ $\bar{p}$ q $\bar{r}$ ...
6. ⌡ r q ...
7. ⌡ $\bar{p}$ q ...
8. q ...

... ...

---

9. $\bar{q}$ ...

... ...

II. *Consolidated Solidity and Validity Proof:*
Supply the derivation column!

| | | |
|---|---|---|
| 1. | $\rfloor\,\rfloor\,\lceil\, p\, q\, \lceil\, \bar{p}\, \bar{r}\, \lceil\, \bar{q}\, \bar{r}$ | |
| 2. | $\bar{\lceil}\, p\, r$ | /∴ $\rfloor\, p\, q$ |
| 3. | ... | 1, O.C. |
| 4. | ... | 3, O.C. |
| 5. | ... | 4, O.C. |
| 6. | ... | 1, O.C. |
| 7. | ... | 6, O.C. |
| 8. | ... | 7, O.C. |
| 9. | ... | 2, CO.Dual. |
| 10. | ... | 5,8, A.A.C. |
| ... | ... | |
| 11. | ... | CFC |
| 12. | ... | 11, CA.Dual. |
| 13. | ... | 12, O.E. |
| ... | ... | |

III. *Consolidated Solidity and Validity Proof:*
Supply the justification column!

| | | |
|---|---|---|
| 1. | $\bigwedge_{xy} \lceil\, Fy\, Gy$ | |
| 2. | $\bigvee_{x} Fx$ | /∴ $\bigwedge_{y} Gy$ |
| 3. | $Fa$ | ... |
| 4. | $\lceil\, Fa\, Ge$ | ... |
| 5. | $Ge$ | ... |
| ... | ... | |
| 2a. | $\overline{\bigwedge_{y}} Gy$ | ... |
| 2b. | $\bigvee_{y} \overline{G}y$ | ... |

| | | |
|---|---|---|
| 2c. | $\bar{G}e$ | ... |
| ... | ... | |

**IV.** *Consolidated Solidity and Validity Proof:*

Supply the derivation column!

| | | |
|---|---|---|
| 1. | $\underset{xyz}{\wedge\wedge\wedge} \rfloor \lceil Fx\ Gy\ Hz$ | |
| 2. | $\int Fa\ Ge$ | |
| 3. | $\underset{xz}{\vee\vee} \lceil Fy\ \bar{H}z$ | /.'. $\underset{yz}{\vee\vee} \lceil Gy\ \bar{H}z$ |
| 4. | ... | 3, P.T. |
| 5. | ... | 4, O.E. |
| 6. | ... | 1, U.T. |
| 7. | ... | 6, I.Dual. |
| 8. | ... | 7, CO.Dual. |
| 9. | ... | 8,5, A.E. |
| 10. | ... | 2, E.Diss., O.E. |
| 11. | ... | 2, E.Diss., O.E. |
| ... | ... | |
| 3a. | ... | CFC |
| 3b. | ... | 3a, P.N. |
| 3c. | ... | 3b, U.T. |
| 3d. | ... | 3c, CU.Dual., O.E. |
| 12. | ... | 10,3d, A.E. |
| ... | ... | |

**V.** *Solidity Proof:*

Supply the justification column!

| | | |
|---|---|---|
| 1. | $\lceil\ \bar{\rceil}\ \bar{p}\ \bar{q}\ p$ | |
| 2. | $\rfloor\ \rfloor\ p\ \bar{q}\ \bar{q}$ | |
| 3. | $p$ | /.'. $\bar{\int}\ p\ q$ |
| 4. | $\rfloor\ \bar{\rceil}\ \bar{p}\ \bar{q}\ \bar{p}$ | ... |

5. $\rfloor \lceil p\ q\ \bar{p}$ ...

6. $\rfloor q\ \bar{p}$ ...

7. $\rfloor \overline{\rceil} p\ \bar{q}\ \bar{q}$ ...

8. $\rfloor \lceil \bar{p}\ q\ \bar{q}$ ...

9. $\rfloor \bar{p}\ \bar{q}$ ...

10. $q$ ...

11. $\bar{q}$ ...

... ...

VI. *Solidity Proof:*

Supply the derivation column!

1. $\bigwedge_{x}\bigwedge_{y} \overline{\rfloor}\ \bar{F}x\ Gy$

2. $\bigwedge_{x}\bigwedge_{y} \rfloor\ Fx\ Gy$ /∴ $\underline{\bigvee_{x} \bar{F}x}$

3. ... 1, U.T.

4. ... 3, CA.Dual., D.N.

5. ... 4, O.E.

6. ... 2, U.T.

7. ... 6, I.Dual.

8. ... 7,5, A.E.

... ...

Solutions:

I. 4. ... 1, I.Dual., D.N.

5. ... 2, U.Dual.

6. ... 3,4, A.C.

7. ... 5,6, A.A.C.

8. ... 4,7, A.A.C.

<u>Solid:</u> F-CF unattainable

9. ... CFC

Valid: 8,9: F-CF

| | | | |
|---|---|---|---|
| II. | 3. | $\rfloor \rfloor \lceil p\ q \lceil \bar{p}\ \bar{r}\ \bar{q}$ | ... |
| | 4. | $\rfloor \rfloor p \lceil \bar{p}\ \bar{r}\ \bar{q}$ | ... |
| | 5. | $\rfloor \rfloor p\ \bar{r}\ \bar{q}$ | ... |
| | 6. | $\rfloor \rfloor \lceil p\ q \lceil \bar{p}\ \bar{r}\ \bar{r}$ | ... |
| | 7. | $\rfloor \rfloor q \lceil \bar{p}\ \bar{r}\ \bar{r}$ | ... |
| | 8. | $\rfloor \rfloor q\ \bar{p}\ \bar{r}$ | ... |
| | 9. | $\rfloor \bar{p}\ \bar{r}$ | ... |
| | 10. | $\bar{r}$ | ... |
| | Solid: | F-CF unattainable | |
| | 11. | $\overline{\rfloor} p\ q$ | ... |
| | 12. | $\lceil \bar{p}\ \bar{q}$ | ... |
| | 13. | $\bar{p}\ ,\ \bar{q}$ | ... |
| | Invalid: | F-CF unattainable | |
| III. | 3. | ... | 2, P.T. |
| | 4. | ... | 1, U.T. |
| | 5. | ... | 4, O.E. |
| | Solid: | F-CF unattainable | |
| | 2a. | ... | CFC |
| | 2b. | ... | 2a, U.N. |
| | 2c. | ... | 2b, P.T. |
| | Valid: | 5,2c: F-CF | |
| IV. | 4. | $\lceil Fi\ \bar{H}o$ | ... |
| | 5. | $Fi\ ,\ \bar{H}o$ | ... |
| | 6. | $\rfloor \lceil Fa\ Gi\ Ho$ | ... |
| | 7. | $\rfloor \overline{\lceil} Fa\ Gi\ Ho$ | ... |
| | 8. | $\rfloor \rfloor \bar{F}a\ \bar{G}i\ Ho$ | ... |
| | 9. | $\rfloor \bar{F}a\ \bar{G}i$ | ... |
| | 10. | $\rfloor \bar{F}a\ Ge$ | ... |

11. $\rfloor\ Fa\ \bar{G}e$ ...

<u>Solid:</u> F-CF unattainable

3a. $\bar{\vee}\vee_{yz} \lceil\ Gy\ \bar{H}z$ ...

3b. $\wedge\wedge_{yz} \bar{\lceil}\ Gy\ \bar{H}z$ ...

3c. $\bar{\lceil}\ Ge\ \bar{H}u$ ...

3d. $Ge\ ,\ \bar{H}u$ ...

12. $\bar{F}a$ ...

Invalid: F-CF unattainable

| | | |
|---|---|---|
| V. | 4. ... | 1, U.Dual. |
| | 5. ... | 4, CA.Dual., D.N. |
| | 6. ... | 5, O.C. |
| | 7. ... | 2, I.Dual. |
| | 8. ... | 7, CA.Dual., D.N. |
| | 9. ... | 8, O.C. |
| | 10. ... | 6,3, A.E. |
| | 11. ... | 9,3, A.E. |

Insolid: 10,11: F-CF

VI.

3. $\bar{\rceil}\ \bar{F}a\ Ge$ ...

4. $\lceil\ Fa\ \bar{G}e$ ...

5. $Fa\ ,\ \bar{G}e$ ...

6. $\rfloor\ Fa\ Ge$ ...

7. $\rfloor\ \bar{F}a\ Ge$ ...

8. $Ge$ ...

Insolid: 5,8: F-CF

## C. *Zetetic Procedures for Legal Reasoning*

Legal reasoning is an activity of the mind supposed to conform to pertinent intellectual and moral standards. An essential task of lawyers is to achieve results of reasoning which can count on general acceptability. The legal reasoner must strive for such conclusions which his colleagues or public authorities would also reach and would thus make decisions anticipated by him. Besides, it is important for him on many occasions that laymen and public opinion approve the results of his reasoning and would adopt them.

In order to secure the tenability of the results of his reasoning, the lawyer must have procedures at his disposal which lend themselves to scrutiny and which are not subject to challenge within the context of particular instances of legal dispute. For securing self-consistency of his reasoning, logical procedures are available to him. Self-consistency is an indispensable but not the sole requirement of rational thought. The strength of legal arguments depends not only on their formal impeccability but also on their material qualities - apart from self-consistency they must possess contentual tenability.

The procedures employed for securing the contentual tenability of reasoning may be called "*zetetic* procedures". The introduction of the terms "zetetic" and "zetetics" is apposite in order to avoid the loose or blurred sense which the words "logical" and "logic" have in ordinary language and frequently even in the language of philosophy. Indeed, in the history of ideas there is a basis for using the word "logic" to refer to all kinds of rational thought or to anything which has something to do with reason (*logos*). However, rational thought has diverse tasks and procedures, which must also be distinguished terminologically in order not to lose sight of their peculiarities, and in order to block the road for smuggling unwarranted commodities of thought. This danger exists where the authority of logic in the strict sense is surreptitiously transferred to those areas in which the cogency of conclusions attainable by stringent reasoning is beyond reach.

The requisite distinction is attempted by means of the phrases "formal logic" and "material logic". However, the use of the same word "logic" in both phrases has a misleading effect. Particularly obnoxious here is the expectation created by the rigour of formal reasoning (characteristic of logic) that *its* cogency can be achieved or claimed also in material reasoning. In contemporary philosophic usage, the word "logic" without any addition normally relates only to formal reasoning; diversions from this practice are generally regarded as curiosities.

The etymological origin of the term "zetetic" is the Greek verb "*zetein*", which means to seek, to investigate, or to inquire; that is, it refers to an intellectual activity whose results cannot be regarded as definite and which is open to continual progress. In modern languages, this word is used very rarely; hence its employment as a technical term with a special sense useful for the theory of reasoning would scarcely give rise to linguistic scruples. Zetetics in the sense to be specified in the following is to be contrasted with dogmatics, which is characterized by fixed opinions. Logic has a dogmatic trait since its principles and methods are relatively established, except in marginal areas, where some problems have not found solutions which can be regarded as definite and where research and search are still going on.

The established logical procedures are such that their results can be regarded as being beyond *any* doubt. In contrast thereto, the results of zetetic procedures can be regarded as no more than being beyond *reasonable* doubt. The dogmatic trait of logic is explainable by the fact that its procedures abstract from the *content* of thought and pertain only to the *framework* of thought. This does not involve any impoverishment of reasoning enterprise, but rather its enrichment with requisite rigour and apposite form. The formal procedures of reasoning constitute only a component of rational thought; they do not curtail contentual thought - contrariwise, they serve it by lending it good order.

There are various kinds of zetetic procedures. All of them represent ways of reasoning which lead to results for which tenability falling short of necessity is claimed - tenability in the sense of probability in some cases and in that of plausibility in others. This claim is strong with some of them, with others it is weak (and can be even very weak). In no case are they compelling; fallibility and refutability are invariably attached to them. However, all of them are examinable reasonings; something resulting from a purposive intellectual effort is achieved by them. They are not mere gropings of the mind nor are they its ridings on purely intuitive brainwaves. The reasoning which is targeted for contentual tenability relates both to judgments about facts and to value judgments as well as to norms. Thus the truth-values are not always pertinent to zetetic procedures of reasoning. Hence, for the conclusions which are achieved or claimed here, the values "true" and "false" are often not appropriate, so that concepts such as "valid" or "tenable" and their negates have to be employed.

The form of the procedures of logical reasoning is expressible in a formula which represents a tautological subjunction. Its antecedent stands for the base of reasoning and its consequent stands for the result of reasoning. The procedure takes place here by application of precepts the compliance with which guarantees the logical necessity of the conclusion; they are axioms or theorems, and rules of derivation. The procedure of logical reasoning is characterized as "*deductive*": the conclusions are *derived* in this procedure. Also the form of the procedures of zetetic reasoning can be conceived as a subjunction. This subjunction represents, however, not a tautology but an amphilogy. The procedure takes place here by application of precepts the compliance with which allows to regard logically possible conclusions as probable or plausible. For the characterization of the procedure of zetetic reasoning I propose the use of the term "*eisductive*": the conclusions are *indicated* (not derived!) in this procedure, which is alluded to by the Greek prefix "eis-".

The eisductive procedures of reasoning can be divided into *exoductive* and *endoductive* procedures. In exoductive procedures, the reasons rendered rest on findings which confront man (as natural, but also as cultural data), whereas in endoductive procedures they rest on findings which lie in men themselves (as their attitudes or inclinations). In the former, the *probability* of conclusions is striven for, in the latter their *plausibility* . Since in the language of philosophy there are not terms available for the given purpose, it was necessary to introduce neologisms again, whose prefixes "exo-" and "endo-" of Greek origin allude to what is meant.

The exoductive procedures of reasoning can further be divided into *reductive* and *interductive* procedures. The reductive procedures aim at the gaining of a principle from a statement or from statements about a datum, whereby the gained principle represents a generalization. The interductive procedures, commonly called "analogy arguments", are concerned with the gaining of a statement about a datum from a statement about another datum, namely on the basis of the similarity which exists between these two data. In reduction, the thought moves from a particular to a general or from a less general to a more general; in interduction, the thought moves from a particular to another particular or from a general to an equally general.

The reductive procedures can be divided into *inductive* and *abductive* procedures. By the inductive procedures, regularities of nature are disclosed, as this happens by the aid of the methods of agreement, difference, residues, or concomitant variations. Here the statements from which the reasoner proceeds are results of the observation of facts.

By the abductive procedures, rules are disclosed, as this happens by the aid of methods which lead to the determination of a *ratio decidendi* or a *ratio legis*. Here the basis of departure consists in the results of the search for meanings of normatively authoritative utterances. In abduction, the methods employed in hermeneutics (i.e. the theory of the disclosure of meanings) play the principal role; the observation of facts has only a subordinate role here. The word "abduction" is occasionally used in ordinary language, but has in it a meaning far removed from the semantic field of zetetics. It also occurs rarely as a term of logic (e.g. to signify a syllogism whose major premiss is certain and whose minor premiss is uncertain). Since its linguistic pre-attachment is scarcely noticeable and its existing uses have no claim to exclusiveness, "abduction" can be introduced as a term to serve useful zetetic purposes. The common feature of inductive and abductive procedures is that they are both reductive. Otherwise they are entirely different. Thus it is advisable to employ a different word for each method.

The interductive procedures can be divided into *paductive* and *geductive* procedures. The (semi-artificial) prefix "pa-" alludes that the thought moves from a particular to another particular. The (semi-artificial) prefix "ge-" alludes that the thought moves from a general to an equally general. With paduction as well as with geduction, it is possible that the statements from which the reasoning proceeds are either results of the observation of facts or results of understanding of normatively authoritative expressions. Notably, there is not only analogy-reasoning relating to findings about nature but also analogy-reasoning relating to norms.

The endoductive procedures can be divided into *eductive* and *perductive* procedures. The essential feature of eductive procedures lies in the application of rules whose observance promotes impartiality, detachment, integrity, clarity, and intelligibility of the fact-situation and the value-situation relevant to the cases of application of eduction. Thus the requisite value-insight is made possible and rendered more acute, and everything disturbing it is reduced or avoided. A decisive importance belongs here to the intellectual or moral "weight" of rendered reasons - this is alluded to by the Greek prefix "eu-". Eduction is a method which today appears under the names of "theory of argumentation", "new rhetoric", "topics", "dialectics", and "paraduction". These names are not quite appropriate because each of them brings out only certain features of euductive procedures or is burdened with meanings which are not relevant to euduction.

Whereas euductive procedures are characterized by the striving for conclusions to which *insightful* assent can be given, the perductive procedures are characterized by the striving for conclusions which *effectively produce assent*. Their aim is not to *convince* but to *persuade* (e.g. by appealing to psychologically effective but nevertheless inapposite compassion or by invoking authorities which are irrelevant for the instant case, however strong these may be otherwise). Perductive arguments are often employed in jury trials. In the counter-argumentation it is to be pointed out that they are not sufficient for the given purposes of reasoning, if they are admissible at all under the pertinent rules of judicial proceedings. That perduction relates to arguments intended merely to persuade is alluded to by the prefix "per-".

In order to complete the system of all basic reasoning procedures, a term is needed which would signify a concept embracing all these procedures. The word "*duction*" would serve the purpose, which means leading to something. In the context of reasoning, it is the conclusion to which all the above specified procedures lead. The prefixes attached to "duction" indicate each specific procedure.

In legal as in other argumentative behaviour, there occur also attempts whose character and aim is to mislead those who are addressed by arguments and to "seduce" them to the acceptance of ideas fancied by and suited to those who advance the arguments. These modes of argumentative behaviour, which may be called "*seductive*", remain outside the system of reasoning procedures, because they are not suited to secure the truth or tenability of claimed conclusions. Their machinations include logical fallacies and contentually irrelevant persuasion tricks actuated by deceitful intention.

Legal reasoning is a total enterprise in which its specific procedures operate as phases or aspects of reasoning; usually they can be separated from each other but only in abstraction. In the performance of concrete tasks of legal reasoning, usually several zetetic procedures are employed. Thus abduction and euduction, induction and interduction, etc., appear frequently as intertwined. Logic is ubiquitously relevant to all these procedures: it is mandatory that no zetetic demarche violates a logical principle. The pointing out of a logical contradiction within an argument effects its refutation in all instances. With all procedures of reasoning, the pointing out of a violation of any basic rule which governs the procedure effects the refutation of argument. With all procedures of reasoning, there are also cases of undecidability. Thus undecidability is encountered in deduction; it can also occur in induction, euduction, etc.

From what has been said above, it is plain that the endoductive procedures of reasoning - both euduction and perduction - have characteristics which make them far removed from the logical procedures of reasoning, if "logic" is to retain the strict sense in which this word is generally used in contemporary philosophy. The extension of the semantic field of "logic" to endoduction, to which also some legal theorists are inclined, is undue and the examples of the corresponding practice do not deserve to be followed.

The basic procedures of reasoning can be represented diagrammatically as follows:

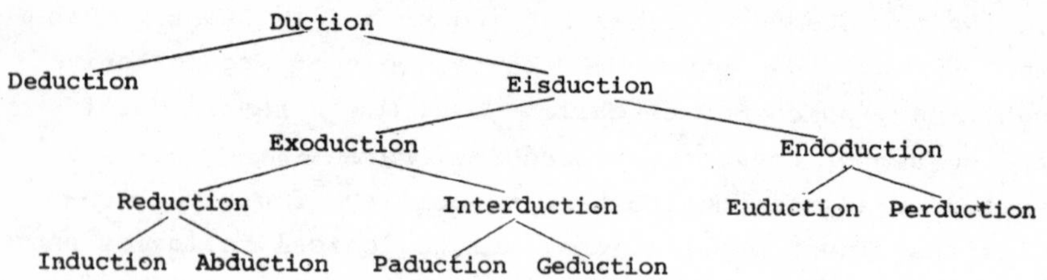


*D. A Manifesto of Legal Logic*

The nature and role of legal logic can be epitomized in the form of the following manifesto:

(1) Legal logic is indispensable for any rational treatment of legal problems.

(2) Legal logic is complementary to other disciplines of fundamental legal thought.

(3) Legal logic is not a source of the material contents of law but an instrument of legal thought.

(4) Legal logic is a prerequisite of utilization of modern technology in the field of law.

(5) Legal logic is indispensable for promoting expediency, efficiency, and integrity of legal reasoning.

## Selected Bibliography


Ackermann, W., *Solvable Cases of the Decision Problem* (1954, new impr. 1962).

Alchourrón, C. & Bulygin, E., *Normative Systems* (1971).

Aldrich, V., "Do Commands Express Propositions?" (1943) 40 *The Journal of Philosophy* 654 ff.

Allen, L.E., "Deontic Logic" (May 1960) *Modern Uses of Logic in Law* 13 ff.

- "Modern Logic. A Useful Language of Lawyers" in Jones, A. (ed.), *Law and Electronics* (1962) ch.3.
- "Some Uses of Symbolic Logic in Law Practice" (1962) 8 *Practical Lawyer* 7 ff.
- "Symbolic Logic: A Razor-Edged Tool for Drafting and Interpreting Legal Documents" (1957) 65 *Yale Law Journal* 833 ff.
- *WFF'n Proof: The Game of Modern Logic* (2nd ed. 1966).

Allen, L.E. & Caldwell, M.E., "Symbolic Logic and Judicial Decision Making" (1963) 28 *Law and Contemporary Problems* 213 ff.

Allen, L.E. & Orechkoff, G., "Towards More Clarity in Drafting and Interpreting of the Internal Revenue Code" (1957) 25 *Chicago Law Review* 1 ff.

Anderson, A.R., "A Reduction of Deontic Logic to Alethic Modal Logic" (1958) 67 *Mind* 100 ff.

- "On the Logic of 'Commitment'" (1959) 10 *Philosophical Studies* 23 ff.
- "The Formal Analysis of Normative Systems" in Rescher, N. (ed.), *The Logic of Decision and Action* (1967) 147 ff.
- "The Logic of Norms" (1958) 1 *Logique et analyse* 84 ff.

Anderson, A.R. & Moore, O., "The Formal Analysis of Normative Concepts" (1957) 22 *American Sociological Review* 9 ff.

Aomi, J., "The Regulative Function of Logic in Legal Decisions" (1973) 59 *Archiv für Rechts- und Sozialphilosophie* 193 ff.

Apostel, L., "Game Theory and the Interpretation of Deontic Logic" (1960) 3 *Logique et analyse* 70 ff.

Åquist, L., "A Binary Primitive in Deontic Logic" (1962) 5 *Logique et analyse* 90 ff.

- "A New Approach to the Logical Theory of Interrogatives" (1965) 25 *Analysis* 174 ff.
- "Choice-Offering and Alternative-Presenting Disjunctive Commands" (1965) 25 *Analysis* 182 ff.
- "Deontic Logic Based on a Logic of 'Better'" (1963) 16 *Acta Philosophica Fennica* 285 ff.
- "Interpretations of Deontic Logic" (1964) 73 *Mind* 246 ff.

- "Postulate Sets and Decision Procedures for Some Systems of Deontic Logic" (1963) 29 *Theoria* 33 ff.
- "Revised Foundations for Imperative, Epistemic, and Interrogative Logic" (1971) 37 *Theoria* 33 ff.

Bar-Hillel, Y., "Imperative Inference" (1966) 26 *Analysis* 79 ff.

Beading, J.D., "La logique judiciaire et l'avocat" in *La logique judiciaire* (1969) 93 ff.

Beatty, H., "On Evaluating Deontic Logic" (1972) 1 *Journal of Philosophical Logic* 439 ff.

Becker, O., *Einführung in die Logistik,vorzüglich in den Modalkalkül* (1951).
- *Untersuchungen über den Modalkalkül* (1952).

Becker, W.G., "Die reale Norm. Die Rechtsnorm als spezifisches logisches Urteil" in P. Bockelmann *et al.* (eds.), *Festschrift für Karl Engisch zum 70. Geburtstag* (1969) 161 ff.

Bergström, L., "Imperative and Contradiction" (1970) 79 *Mind* 421 ff.

Berlet, W., *Das Verhältnis von Sollen, Dürfen und Können* (1968).

Betancour, C., "Les premiers principes logiques de l'impératif" (1965) Beiheft 41 (N.F.4) *Archiv für Rechts- und Sozialphilosophie* 27 ff.

Beth, E.W., *Formal Methods* (1962).

Black, E.W., *Critical Thinking* (1952).

Blanché, R., *L'axiomatique* (1955).
- *Structures intellectuelles* (1966).

Boasson, Ch., "The Use of Logic in Legal Reasoning" (1966) 29(3) *Medeelingen der Koninklijke Nederlandse Akademie van Wetenschappen (Afd. Letterkunde)* 61 ff.

Bobbio, N., "Considérations introductives sur le raisonnement des juristes" (1954) 8 *Revue internationale de philosophie* 67 ff.
- "Diritto e logica" (1962) 39 *Rivista internazionale di filosofia del diritto* 11 ff.
- "Sul ragionamento dei giuristi" (1955) 1 *Rivista di diritto civile* 3 ff.

Bocheński, I.M., *Formale Logik* (1956).

Bocheński, I.M. & Menne, A., *Grundriß der Logistik* (4th ed. 1973).

Bohnert, H.G., "The Semiotic Status of Commands" (1945) 12 *Philosophy of Science* 302 ff.

Bondy, O., "Logical and Epistemological Problems in Legal Philosophy" (1951) 29 *The Australasian Journal of Philosophy* 81 ff.

Boonin, L., "Concerning the Relation of Logic to Law" (1965) 17 *Journal of Legal Education* 155 ff.

Britzelmeyer, W., "Interpretation von Kalkülen" (1949) 7 *Synthese* 50 ff.

Brkič, J., "Consistency, Completeness and Decidability with respect to the Logic of Law and the Provability of Juristic Arguments" (1973) 59 *Archiv für Rechts- und Sozialphilosophie* 473 ff.
- "The Logic of Imperative Sentences" (1968) 3 *Akten des XIV. Internationalen Kongresses für Philosophie* 33 ff.

Carnap, R., *Meaning and Necessity* (1947).
- *The Formalization of Logic* (1943)
- *The Logical Syntax of Language* (1937).

Castañeda, H.N., "Actions, Imperatives, and Obligations" (1967-68) *Proceedings of the Aristotelian Society* 13 ff.
- "Imperative and Deontic Logic" (1958) 19 *Analysis* 42 ff.
- "Imperative Reasonings" (1960-61) 21 *Philosophy and Phenomenological Research* 21 ff.
- "Obligation and Modal Logic" (1960) 3 *Logique et analyse* 40.
- "Outline of a Theory of the General Logical Structure of the Language of Action" (1960) 26 *Theoria* 151 ff.
- "The Logic of Change, Action and Norms" (1965) *The Journal of Philosophy* 333 ff.
- "The Logic of Obligation" (1959) 10 *Philosophical Studies* 17 ff.

Chellas, B., *The Logical Form of Imperatives* (1969).

Chisholm, R., "Contrary-to-Duty Imperatives and Deontic Logic" (1963) 24 *Analysis* 33 ff.

Church, A., "A Note on the Entscheidungsproblem" (1936) 1 *The Journal of Symbolic Logic* 40 ff., 101 ff. ("Correction to a Note on the Entscheidungsproblem").
- *Introduction to Mathematical Logic* (1962).

Clark, R. & Welsh, P., *Introduction to Logic* (1962).

Cobb Jr., Ch.K. & Thompson, D.P., "Law, Logic, and Rationality" (1970) 11 *Jurimetrics Journal* 1 ff.

Cohen, F.S., "Field Theory and Judicial Logic" (1950) 59 *Yale Law Journal* 238 ff.

Cohen, M.R. & Nagel, E., *An Introduction to Logic and Scientific Method* (1934).

Conte, A.G., "Bibliografia di logica giuridica - 1936-1960" in *Atti del V. Congresso Nazionale di Filosofia del Diritto* (1961) 120 ff.
- "Ricerca di un paradosso deontico" (1974) 51 *Rivista internazionale di filosofia del diritto* 481 ff.
- *Saggio sulla completezza degli ordinamenti giuridici* (1962).
- "Décision, complétude, clôture: A propos des lacunes en droit" (1966) 9 *Logique et analyse* 1 ff.

Copi, I.M., *Introduction to Logic* (2nd ed. 1961).
- *Symbolic Logic* (3rd. ed. 1967).
- *The Theory of Logical Types* (1971).

Cornides, T., *Ordinale Deontik* (1974).

Cossio, C., "La lógica jurídica formal en la concepción egológica" (1959) 93 *La ley* 1 ff.

Davis, J.W. *et al.* (eds.), *Philosophical Logic* (1969).

De Morgan, A., *Formal Logic* (1847).

Di Bernando, G., *Introduzione alla logica dei sistemi normativi* (1972).
- *Logica, norme, azione* (1969).

Dopp, J., *Logiques construites par une méthode de déduction naturelle* (1962).
- *Notions de logique formelle* (1967).

Downing, P.B., "Opposite Conditionals and Deontic Logic" (1961) 70 *Mind* 491 ff.

Dubislav, W. "Zur Unbegründbarkeit der Forderungssätze" (1937) 3 *Theoria* 330 ff.

Duncan-Jones, A.E., "Assertions and Commands" (1952) 42 *Proceedings of the Aristotelian Society* 42 ff.

Eaton, R.M., *General Logic* (1931).

Edwards, P., *The Logic of Moral Discourse* (1955).

Engisch, K., *Logische Studien zur Gesetzesanwendung* (3rd ed. 1963).
- "Über Negationen in Recht und Rechtswissenschaft" in *Grundfragen der gesamten Rechtswissenschaft: Festschrift für H. Henkel* (1974) 47 ff.

Esperson, J., "The Logic of Imperatives" (1967) 4 *Danish Yearbook of Philosophy* 57 ff.

Ferrajoli, L., "Saggio di una teoria formalizzata del diritto" (1965) 42 *Rivista internazionale di filosofia del diritto* 55 ff.

Feys, R., "Expression modale du 'devoir-être'" (1955) 20 *The Journal of Symbolic Logic* 91 ff.
- *Modal Logic* (1965).

Fiedler, H., "Juristische Logik in mathematischer Sicht" (1966) 52 *Archiv für Rechts- und Sozialphilosophie* 93 ff.

Fisher, M., "A Logical Theory of Commanding" (1961) 4 *Logique et analyse* 154 ff.
- "A System of Deontic-Alethic Modal Logic" (1962) 71 *Mind* 231 ff.
- "A Three-Valued Calculus for Deontic Logic" *(1961)* 27 *Theoria* 107 ff.
- "On a So-Called Paradox of Obligation" (1962) 59 *The Journal of Philosophy* 23 ff.
- "Strong and Weak Negation of Imperatives" (1962) 28 *Theoria* 196 ff.

Fisk, M., *A Modern Formal Logic* (1964).

Fitch, F.B., "Natural Deduction Rules for Obligations" (1966) 3 *American Philosophical Quarterly* 27 ff.
- *Symbolic Logic* (1952).

Fraassen, B. van, "The Logic of Conditional Obligation" (1972) 1 *Journal of Philosophical Logic* 417 ff.

Frege, G., *Begriffsschrift* (1879).

Frey, G., "Imperativ-Kalküle" in K. Adjukiewicz (ed.), *The Foundation of Statements and Decisions* (1965) 369 ff.

Freytag-Löringhoff, B.v., *Logik: Ihr System und ihr Verhältnis zur Logistik* (4th ed. 1966).

García Máynez, E., *Introducción a la lógica jurídica* (1951).
- *Principios supremos de la ontología formal del derecho y de la lógica jurídica* (1959).
- *Lógica del concepto jurídico* (1959).
- *Lógica del juicio jurídico* (1955).
- *Lógica del raciocinio jurídico* (1964).

Gardies, J.-L., *Essai sur les fondements a priori de la rationalité morale et juridique* (1972).

- "Logique déontique et théorie générale des fonctions complétives" (1973) 16 *Logique et analyse* 143 ff.
- "Une particularité du raisonnement juridique: la présence de fonctions complétives" (1974) 17 *Logique et analyse* 63 ff.

Geach, P., "Imperative and Deontic Logic" (1957) 18 *Analysis* 49 ff.
- "Imperative Inference" (1963) 23 *Analysis* 37 ff.

Gentzen, G., "Untersuchungen über das logische Schließen I und II" (1935) 39 *Mathematische Zeitschrift* 176 ff., 404 ff.

Goble, L.F., "The Iteration of Deontic Modalities" (1966) 9 *Logique et analyse* 197 ff.

Gombay, A., "Imperative Inference and Disjunction" (1965) 25 *Analysis* 58 ff.
- "What Is Imperative Inference?" (1967) 27 *Analysis* 145 ff.

Greenspan, P., "Conditional Oughts and Hypothetical Imperatives" (1975) 72(10) *Journal of Philosophy* 259 ff.

Haag, K. & Wolf, F., *Deontische Logik* (1972).

Hanson, W.H., "A Logic of Commands" (1966) 9 *Logique et analyse* 329 ff
- "Semantics for Deontic Logic" (1965) 8 *Logique et analyse* 329 ff.

Hansson, B., "An Analysis of Some Deontic Logic" (1969) 3 *Nous* 373 ff.

Hare, R.M., *The Language of Morals* (1952).

Hasenjaeger, G., *Einführung in die Grundbegriffe und Grundprobleme der modernen Logik* (1962).

Hermes, H., *Einführung in die mathematische Logik* (1963).

Hilbert, D. & Ackermann, W., *Grundzüge der theoretischen Logik* (5th ed. 1967).

Hilgenheger, N., "Logische Analyse von § 812 Abs.1 BGB" in Rave, D. *et al.* (eds.), *Logische Struktur von Normensystemen am Beispiel der Rechtsordnung* (1971) 103 ff.

Hiller, J.C., "Two Examples of Syntactic Ambiguities in International Agreements" (June 1962) *Modern Uses of Logic in Law* 72 ff.

Hilpinen, R. (ed.), *Deontic Logic: Introductory and Systematic Readings* (1971).

Hintikka, J., *Models for Modalities* (1969).

Hofstadter, A. & McKinsey, J., "On the Logic of Imperatives" (1939) 6 *Philosophy of Science* 446 ff.

Holmes, R.L., "Negation and the Logic of Deontic Assertions" (1967) 10 *Inquiry* 89 ff.

Horovitz, J., *Law and Logic: A Critical Account of Legal Argument* (1972).

Hughes, G.E. & Londey, D.G., *The Elements of Formal Logic* (1965).

Iwin, A.A., "Grundprobleme der deontischen Logik" in Wessel, H. (ed.) *Quantoren - Modalitäten - Paradoxien* (1972) 402 ff.

Jaśkowski, S., "On the Rules of Supposition in Formal Logic" (1934) 1 *Studia logica* 5 ff.

Jørgensen, J., "Imperatives and Logic" (1937-38) 7 *Erkenntnis* 288 ff.

- "Imperatives and Logic" (1969) 6 *Danish Yearbook of Philosophy* 9 ff.

Kahane, H., *Logic and Philosophy* (2nd ed. 1973).

Kalinowski, G., "De la spécificité de la logique juridique" (1966) 11 *Archives de philosophie du droit* 7 ff.
- "Du métalanguage en logique: Réflexions sur la logique déontique et son rapport avec la logique des normes" (1975) 48 série A *Documents de Travail et pré-publications* (Centro Internazionale di Semiotica e di Linguistica, Università di Urbino, Italia) 1 ff.
- *La logique des normes* (1972).
- "Le raisonnement juridique et la logique juridique" (1970) 13 *Logique et analyse* 3 ff.
- "Les thèmes actuels de la logique déontique" (1965) 17 *Studia logica* 75 ff.
- "Logica del diritto: Lineamenti generali" in *Enciclopedia del diritto* (1975) 7 ff.
- "Norms and Logic" (1973) 18 *The American Journal of Jurisprudence* 165 ff.
- "Obligation dérivée et logique déontique relationelle" (1964) 5 *Notre Dame Journal of Formal Logic* 181 ff.
- "Sur quelques suggestions en logique modale et en logique trivalente" (1974) 17 *Logique et analyse* 111 ff.
- "Sur enseignement de la logique dans les facultés de droit" (1970) 15 *Archives de philosophie du droit* 315 ff.
- "Un aperçu élémentaire des modalités déontiques" (1976) 43 *Languages* 10 ff.

Kalinowski, G. & Gardies, J.-L., "Un logicien déontique avant la lettre: Gottfried Wilhelm Leibniz" (1974) 60 *Archiv für Rechts- und Sozialphilosophie* 79 ff.

Kamlah , W. & Lorenzen, P., *Logische Propädeutik* (1967).

Kanger, S., "Law and Logic" (1972) 38 *Theoria* 105 ff.

Karstendieck, H., "Rechtsfindung nach denklogischen Gesetzen" (1969) *Neue juristische Wochenschrift* 1751 ff.

Kashap, P., "Imperative Inference" (1971) 80 *Mind* 141 ff.

Keene, G., "Can Commands Have Logical Consequences?" (1966) 3 *American Philosophical Quarterly* 57 ff.

Kelsen, H., "Recht, Rechtswissenschaft und Logik" (1966) 52 *Archiv für Rechts- und Sozialphilosophie* 545 ff.
- "Recht und Logik" (1965) 12 *Forum* 421 ff., 495 ff.
- "Recht und Logik. Zur Frage der Anwendbarkeit logischer Prinzipien auf Rechtsnormen" (1967) 14 *Neues Forum* 39 ff.

Kenny, A., "Practical Inference" (1966) 26 *Analysis* 65 ff.

Keuth, H., "Über einige logische Eigenschaften von Rechtsnormen" (1972) 3 *Rechtstheorie* 225 ff.
- *Zur Logik der Normen* (1972).

Keynes, J.N., *Studies and Exercises in Formal Logic* (1906).

Kilian, W., "Mathematische Logik und Recht" in Rave, D. *et al.* (eds.), *Logische Struktur von Normensystemen am Beispiel der Rechtsordnung* (1971) 7 ff.

Klaus, G., *Moderne Logik* (1964).

Kleinknecht, R. & Wüst, E., *Lehrbuch der elementaren Logik*, vol.I (1976).

Klinger, R., "Die logische Struktur der normativ geschlossenen und der normativ offenen Rechtsordnungen" (1969) 55 *Archiv für Rechts- und Sozialphilosophie* 323 ff.

- "The Paradox of Counter-Conditional and Its Dissolution" (1971) 11 *Jurimetrics Journal* 189 ff.

Klug, U., "Bemerkungen zur logischen Analyse einiger rechtstheoretischer Begriffe und Behauptungen" in Käsbauer, M. & Kutschera, F. v. (eds.), *Logik und Logikkalkül: Festschrift für Wilhelm Britzelmeyer zum 70. Geburtstag* (1962) 115 ff.

Kneale, W. & Kneale, M., *The Development of Logic* (1962).

Kneemone, G.I., *Mathematical Logic and Foundations of Mathematics* (1963).

Kutschera, F. v., *Elementare Logik* (1967).

- *Einführung in die Logik der Normen, Werte und Entscheidungen* (1973).

Lachmayer, F., *Grundzüge einer Normentheorie* (1977).

Lambert, K. & Fraassen, B. van, *Derivation and Counterexample* (1972).

Langer, S.K., *An Introduction to Symbolic Logic* (1959).

Leblanc, H. & Wisdom, W.A., *Deductive Logic* (2nd ed. 1976).

Ledent, A., "Le statut logique des propositions impératives" (1942) 8 *Theoria* 262 ff.

Lemmon, E., "Deontic Logic and the Logic of Imperatives" (1966) 8 *Logique et analyse* 39 ff.

Lenk, H. (ed.), *Normenlogik: Grundprobleme der deontischen Logik* (1974).

Leonhard, H.S., "Interrogatives, Imperatives, Truth, Falsity, and Lies" (1959) 26 *Philosophy of Science* 172 ff.

Lewis, I.C. & Langford, C.H., *Symbolic Logic* (1932).

Loevinger, L.J., "An Introduction to Legal Logic" (1952) 27 *Indiana Law Review* 471 ff.

Lorenzen, P., "Die Vollständigkeit einer unverzweigten Variante des 'analytischen' Entscheidungsverfahrens der klassischen Logik" (1976) 18 *Archiv für mathematische Logik und Grundlagenforschung* 19 ff.

- *Normative Logic and Ethics* (1969).

Lorenzen, P. & Schwemmer, O., *Konstruktive Logik, Ethik und Wissenschaftstheorie* (1973).

Łukasiewicz, J., *Aristoteles' Syllogistic from the Standpoint of Modern Formal Logic* (2nd ed. 1957).

MacKay, A.F., "Inferential Validity and Imperative Inference Rules" (1969) 29 *Analysis* 145 ff.

Magni, C., "Logica, matematica e scienza giuridica" (1950) 61 *Il diritto ecclesiastico* 193 ff.

- "Per i rapporti fra logica giuridica e moderna sintassi logica" (1952-53) 89 *Rivista italiana per le scienze giuridiche* 62 ff.

Mally, E., *Grundgesetze des Sollens* (1926). New impression in Wolf, K. & Weingartner, P. (eds.), *Ernst Mally: Logische Schriften* (1971).

Mans Puigarnau, J., *Lógica para las juristas* (1969).

Mathieu, V., "Sistemi logici e sistemi giuridici: Impossibilità di autofondazione formale" (1970) 47 *Rivista internazionale di filosofia del diritto* 225 ff.

Mayo, B. & Mitchell, B., "Varieties of Imperatives" (1957) 31 (Suppl.) *Proceedings of the Aristotelian Society* 161 ff.

McLaughlin, R., "Further Problems of Derived Obligations" (1955) 64 *Mind* 400 ff.

Menger, K., "A Logic of Doubtful: On Optative and Imperative Logic" (1939) 1(2) *Reports of a Mathematical Colloquium* 53 ff.

Montrose, J.L., "Syntactic (Formerly Amphibolous) Ambiguity" (June 1962) *Modern Uses of Logic in Law* 65 ff.

Moore, R., "Legal Permission" (1973) 59 *Archiv für Rechts- und Sozialphilosophie* 327 ff.

Moritz, M., "Das sog. Ross'sche Paradox - Interpretation und Kritik" in *Insikt och handling* (1973) 126 ff.
- "Der praktische Syllogismus und das juristische Denken" (1954) 20 *Theoria* 78 ff.
- "Kann das (richterliche) Urteil deduziert werden?" in *Festskrift till Per Olof Ekelöf* (1972) 499 ff.
- "Kann man aus imperativen Prämissen einen indikativen Schlußsatz ableiten?" (1973) B-126 *Annales Universitatis Turkuensis* 143 ff.
- "Permissive Sätze, Erlaubnissätze und deontische Logik" in *Philosophical Essays Dedicated to Gunnar Aspelin on the Occasion of His Sixty-Fifth Birthday* (1963) 108 ff.
- *Über Hohfelds System der juristischen Grundbegriffe* (1960).

Morscher, E., "A Matrix Method for Deontic Logic" (1971) 2 *Theory and Decision* 16 ff.
- "Betrachtungen zur Prädikationenlogik" in Tammelo, I. & Schreiner, H., *Grundzüge und Grundverfahren der Rechtslogik*, vol.II (1977).

Morscher, E. & Zecha, G., "Wozu deontische Logik?" (1972) 58 *Archiv für Rechts- und Sozialphilosophie* 363 ff.

Mott, P., "On Chisholm's Paradox" (1973) 2 *Journal of Philosophical Logic* 179 ff.

Moutafakis, N., *A Logic of Normatives* (1968).

Mullock, Ph., "'Saving' the Hohfeldian Privilege" (1977) 63 *Archiv für Rechts- und Sozialphilosophie* 255 ff.
- "The Hohfeldian Jural Opposites" (1971) 13 *Ratio* 158 ff.
- "The Hohfeldian No-Right: a Logical Analysis" (1970) 56 *Archiv für Rechts- und Sozialphilosophie* 265 ff.
- "The Stone-Tammelo Deontic Logic" (1975) 18 *Logique et analyse* 65 ff.

Murphy, J., "Law and Logic" (1967) 77 *Ethics* 193 ff.

Nozick, R. & Routhlay, R., "Escaping the Good Samaritan Paradox" (1962) 71 *Mind* 377 ff.

Opałek, K., "Les normes, les énoncés sur les normes et les propositions déontiques" (1972) 17 *Archives de philosophie du droit* 355 ff.

- "On the Logical-Semantical Structure of Directives" (1970) 13 *Logique et analyse* 169 ff.
- "On Weak and Strong Permissions" (1973) 4 *Rechtstheorie* 169 ff.

Opfermann, W., "Über einen allgemeinen normlogischen Transformationskalkül und sich daraus ergebende Unmöglichkeitsbeweise" (1972) 3 *Rechtstheorie* 191 ff.

Oppenheim, F., "Outline of a Logical Analysis of Law" (1944) 11 *Philosophy of Science* 142 ff.

Patterson, E.W., "Logic in the Law" (1942) 90 *University of Pennsylvania Law Review* 875 ff.

Peklo, B., "Ein Versuch um weitere formale Ausbildung der deontischen Modallogik" (1975) 16 *Notre Dame Journal of Formal Logic* 71 ff.
- "How and When We Meet Logical Elements in Jurisprudence?" (1974) 51 *Rivista internazionale di filosofia del diritto* 95 ff.
- "Observations on the Construction of Legal Logic" (1972) 58 *Archiv für Rechts- und Sozialphilosophie* 185 ff.
- "Sind die deontischen Funktoren distributiv?" (1974) 15 *Notre Dame Journal of Formal Logic* 301 ff.
- "Über Normeninferenzen" (1964) 7 *Logique et analyse* 203 ff.

Perelman, Ch., *Cours de logique* (1st fasc., 9th ed. 1966), (2nd fasc., 8th ed. 1965), (3rd fasc., 10th ed. 1968).
- *Logique et morale* (1969)

Perelman, Ch. (ed.), *Le raisonnement juridique et la logique déontique* (1970).

Philipps, L., "Aufgaben und Wertungen als Gegenstände der Logik" (1970) Beiheft 6 (N.F.) *Archiv für Rechts- und Sozialphilosophie* 69 ff.
- Braucht die Rechtswissenschaft eine deontische Logik?" in Jahr, G. & Maihofer, W. (eds.), *Rechtstheorie: Beiträge zur Grundlagendiskussion* (1971) 352 ff.
- "Rechtliche Regelung und formale Logik" (1964) 50 *Archiv für Rechts- und Sozialphilosophie* 317 ff.
- "Sinn und Struktur der Normlogik" (1966) 52 *Archiv für Rechts- und Sozialphilosophie* 195 ff.

Podlech, A., "Logische Anforderungen kybernetischer Systeme in ihrer Anwendung auf Rechtssätze" (1968) 23 *Der Betriebsberater* 106 ff.

Prior, A., *Formal Logic* (2nd ed. 1962).
- *Logic and the Basis of Ethics* (1949).
- "Logic, Deontic" in Edwards, P. (ed.) , *The Encyclopaedia of Philosophy*, vol.VI (1967) 509 ff.
- "Modal and Deontic Logic" in Prior, A. (ed.), *Time and Modality* (1957) 140 ff.
- "The Paradox of Derived Obligation" (1954) 63 *Mind* 64 ff.

Prys Williams, A.G., "Law, Logic, and Expectation" (1972) 49 *Rivista internazionale di filosofia del diritto* 315 ff.

Puy Muñoz, F., "El problema de la lógica jurídica" (1963) 10 *Anuario de filosofía de derecho* 51 ff.

Quine, W.V., *Elementary Logic* (2nd ed. 1965).
- *From a Logical Point of View* (2nd ed. 1961).
- *Methods of Logic* (2nd ed. 1958).

Rand, R., "Logik der Forderungssätze" (1939) 1(N.S.) *Revue internationale de la théorie du droit* 308 ff.

- "The Logic of Demand-Sentences" (1962) 14 *Synthese* 237 ff.

Reisinger, L., "Probleme der Symbolisierung und Formalisierung im Recht" in Winkler, G. (ed.), *Rechtstheorie und Rechtsinformatik* (1975) 22 ff.

Rescher, N., "An Axiom System for Deontic Logic" (1958) 9 *Philosophical Studies* 27 ff.

- "Conditional Permission in Deontic Logic" (1962) 13 *Philosophical Studies* 1 ff.
- "Semantic Foundations for Conditional Permission" (1967) 18 *Philosophical Studies* 56 ff.
- *The Logic of Commands* (1966).

Rescher, N. & Robinson, J., "Can One Infer Commands from Commands?" (1964) 24 *Analysis* 1976 ff.

Resnik, M.D., *Elementary Logic* (1970).

Rinaldi, F., "And/or - a Weak Disjunction?" (1964) *The Australian Lawyer* 83 ff.

- "Dilemmas and Circles in the Law" (1965) 51 *Archiv für Rechts- und Sozialphilosophie* 319 ff.
- "Prolegomeni ad una logica del discorso valutativo" (1966) 5 *Università degli Studi di Genova, Annali della Facoltà di Giurisprudenza* 67 ff.

Robinson, J., "Further Difficulties for Conditional Permission in Deontic Logic" (1967) 18 *Philosophical Studies* 27 ff.

Rödig, J., *Die Denkform der Alternative in der Jurisprudenz* (1969).

- "Über die Notwendigkeit einer besonderen Logik der Normen" (1972) 2 *Jahrbuch für Rechtssoziologie und Rechtstheorie* 163 ff.

Ross, A., *Directives and Norms* (1968).

- "Imperatives and Logic" (1944) 11 *Philosophy of Science* 30 ff.
- "On Self-Reference and a Puzzle in Constitutional Law" (1969) 78 *Mind* 1 ff.

Ross, W.D. (ed.), *Aristotle's Prior and Posterior Analytics* (1949).

Russell, B., *The Principles of Mathematics* (2nd ed. 1937).

- *Logic and Knowledge* (ed. by R.C. Marsh, 1956).

Salmon, W.C., *Logic* (1963).

Savigny, E. von, *Grundkurs im logischen Schließen. Übungen zum Selbststudium* (1976).

- "Zur Rolle der deduktiv-axiomatischen Methode in der Rechtswissenschaft" in Jahr, G. & Maihofer, W. (eds.), *Rechtstheorie: Beiträge zur Grundlagendiskussion* (1971) 315 ff.

Schlink, B., "On a Principle of Contradiction in Normative Logic and Jurisprudence" (1971) 2 *Decision* 35 ff.

Schmill, U., "Consideraciones semánticas sobre lógica deóntica, con especial referencia a la jurisprudencia" (1976) 8 *Crítica* 55 ff.

Schneider, E., *Logik für Juristen* (2nd ed. 1972).

Scholz, H., *Geschichte der Logik* (1931).

Scholz, H. & Hasenjaeger, G., *Grundzüge der mathematischen Logik* (1961).

Schreiber, R., *Logik des Rechts* (1962).

Schreiner, H., "Zur rechtslogischen Formalisierung von Normen" (1976) 62 *Archiv für Rechts- und Sozialphilosophie* 365 ff.

Segerstedt, T.T., "Imperative Propositions and Judgments of Value" (1945) 11 *Theoria* 1 ff.

Sellars, W., "Reflections on Contrary-to-Duty Imperatives" (1967) 1 *Nous* 303 ff.

Simco, N.D. & James, G.G., *Elementary Logic* (1976).

Simitis, S., "Das Problem einer juristischen Logik" (1960-61) 3 *Ratio* 52 ff.

Sinclair, W.A., *The Traditional Formal Logic* (5th ed. 1951).

Slupecki, J. et al., "The Theory of Rejected Propositions", Pt. I (1971) 29 *Studia logica* 73 ff., Pt. II (1972) 30 *Studia logica* 97 ff.

Söder, K., *Grundriß der elementaren Logik: Eine Einführung für Juristen* (1968).
- *Formale Logik für Juristen* (1966).

Sosa, E., "On Practical Inference and the Logic of Imperatives" (1966) 32 *Theoria* 211 ff.
- "On Practical Inference with an Excursus on Theoretical Inference" (1970) 13 *Logique et analyse* 213 ff.
- "The Logic of Imperatives" (1966) 32 *Theoria* 224 ff.
- "The Semantics of Imperatives" (1967) 4 *American Philosophical Quarterly* 57 ff.

Stebbing, S., *A Modern Introduction to Logic* (1945).

Stenius, E., "The Principles of a Logic of Normative Systems" (1963) 16 *Acta philosophica fennica* 247 ff.

Storer, T., "The Logic of Value Imperatives" (1946) 13 *Philosophy of Science* 25 ff.

Stranzinger, R., "Der Normbegriff bei Hans Kelsen" (1977) 63 *Archiv für Rechts- und Sozialphilosophie* 400 ff.
- "Die Paradoxa der deontischen Logik" in Tammelo, I. & Schreiner, H., *Grundzüge und Grundverfahren der Rechtslogik*, vol. II (1977) 142 ff.

Strawson, P.F., *Introduction to Logical Theory* (1952).

Strawson, P.F. (ed.), *Philosophical Logic* (1967).

Studnicki, F., "On Completeness and Conclusiveness of Normative Systems" (1973) 59 *Archiv für Rechts- und Sozialphilosophie* 305 ff.

Summers, R., "A Note on Symbolic Logic and the Law" (1961) 13 *The Journal of Legal Education* 46 ff.

Suppes, P., *Introduction to Logic* (1957).

Tammelo, I., "Logical Aspects of the Non-Liquet Controversy in International Law" (1974) 5 *Rechtstheorie* 1 ff.
- "On the Construction of a Legal Logic in Retrospect and in Prospect" (1974) 60 *Archiv für Rechts- und Sozialphilosophie* 377 ff.

- "On the Logical Openness of Legal Orders" (1959) 8 *American Journal of Comparative Law* 187 ff.
- *Outlines of Modern Legal Logic* (1969).
- "Potentialities and Perspectives of Formal Legal Reasoning" in Dorsey, G. (ed.), *Equality & Freedom* (1977) 531 ff.
- *Rechtslogik und materiale Gerechtigkeit* (1971).
- "The Antinomy of Parliamentary Sovereignty" (1958) 44 *Archiv für Rechts- und Sozialphilosophie* 495 ff.

Tammelo, I. & Klinger, R., "The Counter-Formula Method and Its Applications in Legal Logic" in Fischer, M. *et al.* (eds.), *Dimensionen des Rechts: Gedächtnisschrift für René Marcic* (1974) 349 ff.

Tammelo, I. & Moens, G., *Logische Verfahren der juristischen Begründung* (1976).

Tammelo, I. & Schreiner, H., *Grundzüge und Grundverfahren der Rechtslogik*, vol.I (1974), vol.II (1977).

Tammelo, I. & Schreiner, H. (eds.), *Strukturierungen und Entscheidungen im Rechtsdenken* (1978).

Tarski, A., *Logic, Semantics, Metamathematics* (transl. by J.H. Woodger, 1956).

Tarski, A. *et al.* (eds.), *Undecidable Theories* (1953).

Thomas, J.A., *Symbolic Logic* (1977).

Thomason, R.H., *Symbolic Logic. An Introduction* (1970).

Vetter, H., "Deontic Logic without Deontic Operators" (1971) 2 *Theory and Decision* 67 ff.

Wagner, H. & Haag, K., *Die moderne Logik in der Rechtswissenschaft* (1970).

Watts, I., *Logic* (1970).

Wedeking, G., "Are there Command Arguments?" (1969) 30 *Analysis* 161 ff.

Weinberger, O., "Einige Betrachtungen über die Rechtsnormen vom Standpunkt der Logik und Semantik" (1964) 7 *Logique et analyse* 212 ff.
- "Der Erlaubnisbegriff und der Aufbau der Normenlogik" (1973) 16 *Logique et analyse* 113 ff.
- "Fundamental Problems of the Theory of Legal Reasoning" (1972) 58 *Archiv für Rechts- und Sozialphilosophie* 305 ff.
- "Normenlogik anwendbar im Recht" (1970) 13 *Logique et analyse* 93 ff.
- "Normenlogik und Rechtstheorie" (1968) 2 *Akten des XIV. Internationalen Kongresses für Philosophie* (1968) 297 ff.
- *Philosophische Studien zur Logik* (1964).
- *Rechtslogik: Versuch einer Anwendung moderner Logik auf das juristische Denken* (1970).
- *Studien zur Normenlogik und Rechtsinformatik* (1974).
- "The Conception of Non-Satisfaction and Deontic Logic" (1972) 14 *Ratio* 16 ff.
- "Über die Negation von Sollsätzen" (1957) 23 *Theoria* 102 ff.
- "Über die Offenheit des rechtlichen Normensystems" in *Walter Wilburg: Zum 70. Geburtstag* (1975) 439 ff.

Weingartner, P., "A Predicate Calculus for Intensional Logic" (1973) 2 *Journal of Philosophical Logic* 220 ff.

Whitehead, A.N. & Russell, B., *Principia Mathematica*, 3 vols. (2nd ed. 1925-27).

Williams, B., "Imperative Inference" (1963) 23 *Analysis* 30 ff.

Wittgenstein, L., *Tractatus Logico-Philosophicus* (with English translation 1922).

Wolfers, A., *Logische Grundformen der juristischen Interpretation* (1971).

Wright, G.H. von, "A New System of Deontic Logic" (1964) 1 *Danish Yearbook of Philosophy* 173 ff. Correction of the System (1965) 2 *Danish Yearbook of Philosophy* 103 ff.
- *An Essay on Deontic Logic and the General Theory of Action* (2nd ed. 1972).
- "A Note on Deontic Logic and Derived Obligation" (1956) 65 *Mind* 57 ff.
- *An Essay on Modal Logic* (1951).
- "Deontic Logic" (1951) 60 *Mind* 1 ff.
- "Deontic Logic" (1967) 4 *American Philosophical Quarterly* 136 ff.
- "Deontic Logic and the Ontology of Norms" (1968) 2 *Akten des XIV. Internationalen Kongresses für Philosophie* (1968) 304 ff.
- "Deontic Logic and the Theory of Conditions" in Hilpinen, R. (ed.), *Deontic Logic: Introductory and Systematic Readings* (1971) 159 ff.
- "Deontic Logic Revisited" (1973) 4 *Rechtstheorie* 37 ff.
- "Handlungslogik" in Lenk, H. (ed.), *Normenlogik: Grundprobleme der deontischen Logik* (1974) 9 ff.
- *Handlung, Norm und Intention. Untersuchungen zur deontischen Logik* (edited and introduced by Hans Poser, 1977).
- *Logical Studies* (1957).
- *Norm and Action* (1963).
- "Normenlogik" in Lenk, H. (ed.), *Normenlogik: Grundprobleme der deontischen Logik* (1974) 25 ff.
- "The Logic of Practical Discourse" in Klibansky, R. (ed.), *Contemporary Philosophy: A Survey* (1968) 141 ff.

Wróblewski, J., "Axiomatization of Legal Theory" (1972) 49 *Rivista Internazionale di filosofia del diritto* 380 ff.
- "The Problem of the Meaning of the Legal Norm" (1964) 14 *Österreichische Zeitschrift für öffentliches Recht* 253 ff.

Zermelo, E., "Untersuchungen über die Mengenlehre I" (1908) 65 *Mathematische Annalen* 261 ff.

Ziemba, Z., "Deontic Syllogistic" (1970) 28 *Studia logica* 139 ff.

Ziembiński, Z., "Conditions préliminaires de l'application de la logique déontique dans les raisonnements juridiques" (1970) 13 *Logique et analyse* 107 ff.
- "Le language du droit et la language juridique: Les critères de leur discernement" (1974) 19 *Archives de philosophie du droit* 25 ff.
- "Les lacunes de la loi dans le système juridique polonais contemporain et les méthodes utilisées pour les combler" in Perelman, Ch. (ed.), *Études de logique juridique* (1960) 38 ff.
- *Practical Logic* (1976).

INDEX